Sisters in Mourning

Sisters in Mourning

Daughters Reflecting on Care, Loss, and Meaning

Edited by
SU YON PAK
and MYCHAL B. SPRINGER

Foreword by MARY GORDON

CASCADE *Books* • Eugene, Oregon

SISTERS IN MOURNING
Daughters Reflecting on Care, Loss, and Meaning

Copyright © 2021 Wipf and Stock Publishers. All rights reserved. Except for brief quotations in critical publications or reviews, no part of this book may be reproduced in any manner without prior written permission from the publisher. Write: Permissions, Wipf and Stock Publishers, 199 W. 8th Ave., Suite 3, Eugene, OR 97401.

Cascade Books
An Imprint of Wipf and Stock Publishers
199 W. 8th Ave., Suite 3
Eugene, OR 97401

www.wipfandstock.com

PAPERBACK ISBN: 978-1-7252-9137-9
HARDCOVER ISBN: 978-1-7252-9127-0
EBOOK ISBN: 978-1-7252-9129-4

Cataloging-in-Publication data:

Names: Pak, Su Yon, editor. | Springer, Mychal B., editor. | Gordon, Mary, foreword.

Title: Sisters in mourning : daughters reflecting on care, loss, and meaning / edited by Su Yon Pak and Mychal B. Springer ; foreword by Mary Gordon.

Description: Eugene, OR: Cascade Books, 2021. | Includes bibliographical references and index.

Identifiers: ISBN: 978-1-7252-9137-9 (paperback). | ISBN: 978-1-7252-9127-0 (hardcover). | ISBN: 978-1-7252-9129-4 (ebook).

Subjects: LCSH: Pastoral theology. | Mothers and daughters—United States. | Death—Psychological aspects. | Mourning.

Classification: BL65 S18 2021 (print). | BL65 (epub).

To Our Mothers

Mary Breitman
17 April 1914—16 June 2007

Gladys Isabelle Jackson
28 November 1921—16 December 2008

Louise Consuelo Marquez Jaramillo
12 October 1917—22 March 2009

Kim (Pak) Yang Sook
12 April 1927—14 March 2017

Marilyn D'elia O'Loughlin
3 March 1939—13 May 1982

Tova Springer
27 November 1930—27 February 2017
7 Kislev 5691—1 Adar 5777

Bess Merola Talvacchia
20 November 1920—19 June 1978

Contents

Permissions | viii
Foreword | ix
Acknowledgments | xi
Introduction | xiii
Who We Are | xviii

PART I: CARING

1. This Old Woman Is Not What You Think | 3
   BARBARA EVE BREITMAN

2. Stretching without Breaking | 19
   KATHLEEN T. TALVACCHIA

3. Caring for Babygirl | 35
   CARI JACKSON

4. *No Digas Nada* (Don't Say Anything) | 49
   LINDA JARAMILLO

INTERLUDE: PICTURING OUR MOTHERS | 65

PART II: GRIEVING

5. A Voice Calling Back | 73
   LAURA O'LOUGHLIN

6. Fragmented Souvenir: Witnessing a Life | 91
   SU YON PAK

7. Satisfy Us with Your Goodness: Caring and Grieving for My Mother, Tova | 111
   MYCHAL B. SPRINGER

Resources | 125

Permissions

Translation of *The Thunder: Perfect Mind*, by Hal Taussig et al. in *A New New Testament*. Permission granted by Hal Taussig.

Tanakh: A New Translation of The Holy Scriptures according to the Traditional Hebrew Text (Philadelphia: The Jewish Publication Society, 1985).

New Revised Standard Version (NRSV), copyright © 1989 National Council of Churches of Christ.

King James Version (KJV). New York: American Bible Society, 1982.

Ubbiri, "The Earth" from *The First Free Women: Poems of the Early Buddhist Nuns* by Matty Weingast. Copyright © 2020 by Matty Weingast. Reprinted by arrangement with The Permissions Company, LLC on behalf of Shambhala Publications Inc., Boulder, CO, www.shambhala.com.

"This Old Woman Is Not What I Think. . ." originally published in *Mother to Daughter, Daughter to Mother, Mothers on Mothering: A Day Book and Reader*. Edited by Tillie Olson. Old Westbury, New York: The Feminist Press, 1984. Used with permission granted by Betsy Sholl.

"We Never Said Goodbye." Used with permission granted by Joy Bokshin Lee Gebhard.

Jill Nathanson, *Cadence*, 2017, photograph by Roz Akin, courtesy of the artist.

Foreword

OF ALL THE THREADS in the family carpet, the mother/daughter is arguably the knottiest. In myth and fiction, it has not received nearly the attention of the father/son thread (think Zeus and Cronus, think Oedipus) or the mother/son thread (think Orestes and Clytemnestra, think D. H. Lawrence). The mother/daughter story in Greek myth has much more nuance and ambivalence than is customary: the fate of Demeter and Persephone is perennially unresolved—the daughter must travel back and forth from the mother's embrace, spending half the year with her dark ravisher, her mother having received even that partial reprieve by threatening the death of the planet. Often the specter of the Hades figure renders the relationship even more fraught. If, as has been the case for most of history, the daughter's fate is inextricably connected to her chastity, the mother feels the crushing pressure of being the guardian of the daughter's sexuality. In modern and even postmodern family life, the mother has been in charge of home and hearth, the father the citizen of the larger world, coming home from work to kiss the bathed, fed children goodnight, whereas the mother has had the sometimes-frustrating work of feeding and bathing. All too frequently, the father gets the glamour role, the mother that of the enforcer.

The knot becomes even knottier when the tables are turned and the daughter becomes in relation to the mother not the cared for but the carer. Women are far more likely to be given the role of carer when a family member becomes ill or disabled. It is even the case that daughters-in-law are more likely to care for mothers-in-law than sons are for mothers. In a world of dispersed and fragmented families many women are faced with this daunting challenge: how to care for a diminishing mother without losing one's own life. It is this challenge that *Sisters in Mourning* faces head-on.

Sisters in Mourning never falls into the trap of oversimplification. The authors recognize that we live in a racially, ethnically, and class-bound world, in an America that has less concern than ever to provide an adequate safety net. One of its achievements is the acknowledgement of the role of paid caregivers, never adequately compensated for their demanding and often heroic work. And there is no suggestion that the problem of caring for a mother is a one-size-fits-all. Not only do social factors contribute to the differences, but there is a difference that stems from the time in a daughter's life when a mother's disability strikes. For Kathleen T. Talvacchia and Laura O'Loughlin, whose young lives were blighted by their mothers' illnesses and deaths, there is a sense of deprivation that is very different from the experience of Mychal Springer, who had the anguishing problem of her mother's hanging on too long to life when death was clearly, for the guilt-ridden daughter and the life-burdened mother, the desirable outcome. Cari Jackson, who had to come to terms with the fact that her mother never accepted her sexual identity, has a very different response from Linda Jaramillo, who feels that she and her mother left nothing unsaid, and who is moved by a Catholic Latina community—although she has rejected it for herself. Su Yon Pak's almost mystical connection to her dead and dying mother, which has its roots in Korean culture, is not the same thing as Barbara Breitman's, who only in her mother's diminishment understands the racial and familial trauma that her mother has absorbed in her bones, coming to a late comprehension of some of the difficult aspects of her mother's personality. And so, the past hovers over and invades the present and the future for these daughters and drives the work that they must do for healing and forward movement.

The women in *Sisters in Mourning* are women of the spirit, sometimes drawing on the traditions of their birth, sometimes having to steer in new directions. But whatever the path they take, they are not unaccompanied, and this sense of an accompanying presence as a source of hope and sustenance is yet another of the important contributions of this rich and generous collection.

Acknowledgments

THIS WORK OF LOVE began not with me, but with my mother, Kim (Pak) Yang Sook, and the elders of her generation. I am indebted to their capacity to witness life even amid destruction. My father, the late Pak Dong Kyu; my mother's brother, the late Kim Chong Sung and his wife, Kim Chung Ok; her other brother, the late Kim Jong Suk; her sister, Kim (Pyun) Insook; her lifelong friend, the late Kwak Ki-wha; and their larger-than-life or, more aptly, larger-than-death stories accompanied me through my loss and taught me resilience. I am grateful for my life partner and my anchor, Kathy, who has shared the burdens and the gifts of caring, and for her indomitable loving presence (especially her driving skills!) my elders praised. I hope for my siblings—Eugene, Helen, and Serina—that our bond of love can live up to my mother's and her siblings' tenacious love. And to the subsequent generations, my daughter, Jocelyn, son-in-law, Patrick, and our precious granddaughter, Isobel, and my younger daughter, Chloe, and our delightful grandpuppy, Chara, I wish to leave a legacy of fierce devotion that their amazing ancestors exemplified.

My gratitude is boundless—for my mother, Tova Springer; my father, James Springer; my sister, Tamar Springer and the Stancroff tribe; and my brother, Jonathan Springer. They are deeply part of me in how I walk in this world. And for the family I live with today—my two daughters, Ariella and Tali, who inspire me to investigate my life in order to offer it to them as best I can—and my husband, Jonathan, who has oriented me in this world and equipped me to be who I am. And for my mother's brother, Aryeh Livni, and her sister-in-law, Simone Livni—my beloved uncle and aunt—who have been essential from the beginning, together with my cousins. And for the incredible family that became mine through marriage—my second mother, Norma Rosen, sister Anna and the Rosen-Rosens, who are core to my life.

Acknowledgments

This book could not have been birthed without the Sisters who ventured courageously and graciously into this exploration. Their willingness to be open to the unfolding was an affirmation of faith and trust, in us and in each other. We are grateful to the two seminaries, the Jewish Theological Seminary and Union Theological Seminary, that helped to foster our connection. And finally, to K. C. Hanson, our editor at Cascade Books, who received our unconventional ideas with grace and offered direction. We could not have asked for a more supportive guide in publishing this book.

Introduction

OUR MOTHERS PASSED AWAY within weeks of each other. We had both been caring for our mothers with dementia for years. Mychal's mother passed away on Monday, February 27, 2017. The day before, Su had admitted her mother to hospice care. On Tuesday, after visiting her mother, Su and her partner, Kathy, visited Mychal, who was sitting shiva, her apartment packed with people, a powerful ritual of witness and presence. After leaving Mychal's apartment, Su made the dreaded calls to her mother's siblings to let them know that their sister's life on this earth was ending.

Two weeks after Mychal's mother died, Su's mother passed away. "We are sisters in mourning," Mychal wrote to Su. "I feel the sisterhood of our grief and I hope to find a time when we can be together before long. You are a blessing. May your mother's memory be for a blessing, and may you find comfort as you grieve."

We *are* sisters in mourning. But before that, we were colleagues who actively collaborated on various innovative projects and worked across the street from each other, Su at Union Theological Seminary, Mychal at the Jewish Theological Seminary. Caring for our mothers and grieving the loss had created a strong bond between us, connecting us through this shared dimension of our personal lives beyond the professional. The idea for this project came from Su's close colleague Greg Snyder, husband of Laura O'Loughlin, whose mother died when Laura was young. When Su shared with Greg her caring and grieving journey and Mychal's email that we were "sisters in mourning," he said, "Oh, that's a book that needs to be written." This is how our project began.

We knew how essential our experiences of caring and grieving were for us, and we knew that there were other "sisters in mourning," women who had lost their mothers who would be open to joining us on our journey of looking for language and community and ways to explore and integrate the

Introduction

many dimensions of these profound experiences. We began with a commitment to establish a shared space where we could talk about things so central and yet so easy to leave unspoken, relegated to private places. We thought of fabulous women from diverse backgrounds. Su invited Kathy, Laura, and Cari. Mychal invited Bobbi. Cari invited Linda. We asked them if they would like to share their stories and explore these questions with us: What does your culture and spiritual tradition expect of you as a caregiver? How does gender impact this expectation? What do you ask of yourself? And how do these demands shape each other? What is the relationship between the expectations of your community, the caregiving that you actually provide, and the experience of grieving?

The first time we met, in February 2018, the energy was exhilarating. Our simple prompts led us to share stories with depth and passion. Some of us lost our mothers long ago, and for others, the death was still fresh; some of us experienced great turbulence in our relationships with our mothers; some of us had been in years of therapy in which our mothers were central characters. But regardless of where we came from, our group allowed us to explore feelings, puzzles, and nuances that expanded our capacity to dive deeply into our grief work, our healing work. While each sister spoke personally, each story resonated deeply with the others. Each of us had a unique experience and perspective. Sometimes there would be nods of identification, and sometimes awareness of difference. Each telling invited more opening, more unfolding, as we heard one another into speech.[1]

The experience of being a diverse group was essential to each of us in this journey, as we examined points of connection and difference that enriched our understanding of the human experience, the experiences of women in particular, and the life of the spirit. We were a diversity of identities, experiences, spiritualities, and personality styles. For some of us, the realm of emotions was our native ground, but not for all of us. We are Jewish, Buddhist, Protestant, Inter-Spiritual, Double-Belonger, and Catholic. Our ancestries, ethnicities, and identities include Black, White, Latina, Korean, Italian, Irish, Ashkenazi Jewish, and various blends. We are US-born and immigrants. We are straight. We are queer. Some of us are mothers and some of us are not. We are sisters in mourning.

In keeping with grief, our process was not linear or tidy. At times we brought inarticulate feelings and experiences, but the flow back and forth with one another in a space that was hospitable meant that we didn't need

---

1. See Morton, *The Journey Is Home*.

Introduction

to have it all figured out before we spoke, that there was room to share our stuckness and be met there. This process led us to insights we would not have imagined. We were able to integrate our lived experiences in new ways. In describing the experience, one of us said: "This group helped me to birth my grief for my mother." We took up our roles as one another's midwives.

We moved quickly into drafting fragments of chapters, sharing them with one another and receiving feedback. The writing and reflecting, and the feedback we received enabled us to go deeper into understanding what we did not yet understand. For some of us, the writing flowed. For others, it was agonizing, impossible. There were barriers that each of us needed to overcome, the fragmentation caused by trauma, opportunities to gather fragments into a new whole. Through a combination of sharing, stepping back, reflecting, writing, and coming together again, we planted seeds in one another, accepting that some would grow and others would remain dormant.

This book is organized around two practices: caring and grieving. While each section emphasizes one of the practices, the two are inextricably connected. Similarly, while each chapter leads with a certain topic, there are echoes of that topic in other chapters. As is the reality with caring and grieving, the boundaries between one sister's story and another sister's story are semipermeable.

Here are some major themes that arise from the book. The tension between caregiving and self-care, a tension tied to obligation and guilt, shows up in every chapter. These are also gendered expressions, which are further complicated when the relationship between mother and daughter is strained. Trauma (and resilience) and transgenerational transmission of trauma (and resilience) find their way throughout the book. Whether they are sociopolitical traumas, like war, displacement, racism, or genocide, or part of personal experience, like a traumatic death or accidental death, trauma seems embedded in almost every sister's story, affecting our bodies and our spirits. Trauma creates fragmentation. It keeps a part of ourselves separate from other parts of ourselves. It also keeps us from truly knowing our mothers. But when we listen attentively with discerning hearts, these stories of trauma and the transmission of trauma are also stories of resilience and the transmission of resilience. We see our mothers anew. These stories are a testament to how we continue our relationships with our mothers long after their deaths, transforming the mother–daughter bond,

Introduction

however difficult or tenuous it was, even if we could not say goodbye at the time of her death.

It matters in our grieving whether we were able to say goodbye. It also matters whether the rituals—religious and cultural—were available as "medicine for these moments," to quote Laura, "to traverse this sacred journey of death." Whether formal like shiva or informal and everyday like untangling the yarn, rituals can hold us even in the intensity of devastating loss. Grief is complex. But it is more complicated by ambiguous loss when a final goodbye is not possible, as in prolonged losses that dementia brings, or if we could not gather for a funeral due to the COVID-19 pandemic. When death comes out of season (so to speak), when a mother dies at age thirty-eight, with much of her life unlived, or is murdered leaving two young daughters in her cousin's care, grief from unseasonal death haunts us like dangerous and unexpected visitations from the past. The burden is even heavier when we live with difficult end-of-life decisions. But we found that the load is lightened when we share it with a trusted community that participates in midwifing one another's grief.

Each of the sisters took a lead in authoring a chapter in collaboration with the group as a whole. We then invited the thoughts, associations, and spiritual resources of the other sisters to enhance the chapters with our sisterly dialogue. These voices can be heard, shall we say, in textboxes throughout the chapters. An asterisk at the end of a sentence or a phrase alerts readers to look for the textbox that links to the words just read. We encourage you to eavesdrop on our conversation as well as to add your own voice to it.

These themes of caring and grieving are at once universal and particular. They show up in prepandemic, pandemic, and postpandemic times. They are a part of our human condition. However, we realize, that these themes have heightened significance during the COVID-19 pandemic. While none of us has experienced death of our mothers during the COVID-19 pandemic, we have journeyed closely with loved ones, colleagues, and patients who have. We have grappled with death out of season, with the inability to be present during the last hours of loved one's life, with the inability to say goodbye, with ambiguous loss, with complicated family relationships, and with difficult decisions at the end of life—experiences that have been intensified as the virulent contagion attacks every known boundary and life as we know it. It is our hope that wisdom found in these chapters can accompany you toward your healing during this global crisis.

xvi

Introduction

Because we are geographically dispersed, almost all of our work together took place virtually. We did not know when we started that the world would transform onto virtual platforms because of COVID-19, but it seems fitting that as this book heads to publication we are sharing a process that has worked so well on Zoom. The need for spaces in which people can be supported and heard has only increased with social isolation, so we hope that the stories in these chapters and the process that led to the writing of the book might inspire you to connect with a circle of mourners to engage in your own process of discovery and support. We decided to include questions for reflection at the end of each chapter to help you get started.

This book is about memory. It is about what is forgotten, remembered, endangered, recovered, shared, hoarded, hidden, spoken, created, and ritualized. It is about how we remember our mothers, how we remember ourselves as daughters, and how we create memories of our ongoing relationships to our mothers. Though we never stop grieving, we may see our mothers, and thus ourselves, more clearly, more truly.

"What would happen if one woman told the truth about / her life?" Muriel Rukeyser writes, "The world would split open."[2] We know for certain, that telling truths about our lives has split *our* worlds wide open. In these opened spaces, we have healed in ways we did not know we needed. We invite you to join the journey.

---

2. Rukeyser, "Käthe Kollwitz," lines 108–10 (page 462).

Who We Are

Barbara Eve Breitman

My mother was surprised I was so different from her. Growing up in the '60s, I was a hippie dressed like a bohemian, full of protest and poetry. The daughter of impoverished refugees, my mother dressed in classics. In graduate school, I brought her to a lengthy Passover seder at the home of an esteemed professor. She sat politely throughout. But when we left, she blurted out, "Bobbi, this is everything I tried to get away from!" Yet when I won an award in Jewish communal service, she beamed with pride. She would still be surprised to know I became a professor of pastoral care at a rabbinical college (Reconstructionist) and created their program in Jewish spiritual direction.

Cari Jackson

While my mom and I were different in many ways, I am grateful for the ways we were alike. Once when she heard me preach, she said, "You're a preacher and a comedian." We share a deep spiritual connection and a great sense of humor. Because of her love for God and for all people, she was proud when I became an ordained minister in the United Church of Christ and a pastor in varied congregational and community settings. Like my mom did, I am learning to live boldly with passion, dignity, confidence, compassion, and grace. And like her, I live in the courage to reimagine and reinvent myself as I experience new horizons

Who We Are

Linda Jaramillo

Mom would be tickled to know that I have mastered the art of secret keeping and learned the discretionary practice of sharing my truth whenever it feels like the right thing to do. Serving as a national officer of the United Church of Christ taught me that public life in social justice ministry imposes serious limits to our privacy. Since entering my encore years of retirement, I relish in the release of my colonized spirit and courageously claiming the authorship of my own story.

Laura O'Loughlin

While my mother's life was traditional, what she hoped for my future was not. I imagine her great surprise seeing her daughter—raised in a Catholic, Italian-Irish, working-class home—become a psychotherapist and Zen Buddhist teacher. I imagine her relief knowing that in the wake of so much familial loss, her daughter found solace and strength. I imagine her amazement at her shy, elusive child devoting her life to leading and caring for Brooklyn Zen Center, a community grounded in love and justice. That my life is filled with such meaning and joy is a tribute to my mom.

Su Yon Pak

My mother's persistent desire was to run a retreat center. She did manage to open one, against all odds and the advice of her children. Sadly, for various reasons, some spectacular, it had to close. But she never gave up on her dream. The irony is that in discerning my own desires, I came upon a "house-in-the-woods." My dream is to create a space where weary folks could come for contemplation, nourishment, and rest. Whether with my teaching and administering as a theological field educator at Union Theological Seminary, or with running a retreat house, my mother would be pleased.

Mychal B. Springer

A defining moment in my mother's life was when she decided to leave Israel and live in the United States. Growing up I was continually in dialogue with that decision, as I felt the disorientation of exile acutely. I have worked hard to feel at home. For the last three decades my home has been in New York, where I live with my husband, Jonathan Rosen, and my two daughters. I work as the manager of clinical pastoral education at NewYork-Presbyterian Hospital.

Kathleen T. Talvacchia

My mother always said to me in a moment of loving irritation at some mischief or commotion of which I was at the center, that I had the "terrible twos" until I was five. My siblings would likely agree! Had she lived to see me now, she would not be surprised to know that I have honed those skills into the power of "faithful-disruptiveness" as a contextual theologian with interests in practical theology, Christian practices of marginalized communities, and Queer theology.

PART I

Caring

1

This Old Woman Is Not What You Think

Barbara Eve Breitman

It is March 1993. There are blizzard warnings for a superstorm moving up the East Coast. I'm afraid my eighty-year-old mother will be snowed in, alone and unable to fend for herself.

I race up the New Jersey Turnpike from Philadelphia to Dobbs Ferry, New York, so we can get snowed in together. I arrive as the snowfall gets heavier and we watch the intensifying white gusts, listening to television coverage of the advancing storm.

After a while I say, "Okay, Mom. Time to make dinner."

I open the freezer and see nothing but leftover coffee ice cream, packs of frozen vegetables, margarine, frozen orange juice. In the refrigerator are the things that last a long time on the door. The cabinets are almost bare.

"Mom, when's the last time you went shopping?"

"I don't remember."

"Mom, there's almost no food here."

"Don't worry, Bobbi. We'll be all right."

"Mom, I don't think this is all right."

She shrugs her shoulders.

For five days we eat cream of wheat cereal, crackers, frozen vegetables, tuna, and pasta, drink hot tea and orange juice. How had I missed what was happening to her?*

PART I: CARING

How had I missed what was happening to her?

I remember the day when I first asked that question. I lived in Washington, DC, a forty-minute drive from Mom, and visited her often. Yet, one day, I noticed that she was using mailing address labels in places other than envelopes. She was using the labels as tape to secure a phone list of key family and friends onto the wall. I had made that list for her when I noticed that she was having trouble thumbing through her personal address book to find numbers. Since her treasured address book was not working for her anymore, I made an accommodation to make it work. I had missed the full significance of what was happening.

My truth is that I had noticed lots of things along the way, many of which I could easily explain or rationalize. It wasn't until there were no more explanations or rationalizations to help me make sense of or to give me peace about the changes that I fully registered that something big was happening to Mom. Her creative, unorthodox use of the mailing labels jolted me into a new reality—the Mom I had known all my life was fading away.
—Cari

I don't want my mother to see me crying. I take a hot shower and as the water beats down on the porcelain tub, I sob and let myself know.

∾

We never spoke the words "Alzheimer's" or "dementia" between us. For years, my mother was still able to do many things by herself. She washed, bathed, and dressed, kept the kitchen and apartment tidy, watered her plants, watched public television. But during the blizzard, I realized there was a vacancy about her, a "whatever" attitude, the opposite of how she used to be. Always cautious and anxious, she had stopped shopping for food or cooking because, though she could not say so directly, she must have sensed it was too risky.

The mother I knew was meticulous and compulsive. She had been an exacting administrative assistant to the chief financial officer of a large child welfare agency in New York, though she had only a high school diploma. In the 1920s, as a female child of immigrants, she'd been steered into secretarial services because college was not meant for someone like her. But as a highly intelligent, skilled, and dependable professional, she managed the financial office of a complex agency like clockwork.

This Old Woman Is Not What You Think

She ran our home the same way; she could not tolerate anything out of place. Before I got into bed at night, everything had to be in a drawer or closet, on a bookshelf. All surfaces clear. There was only one right way to do everything: make a bed, set a table, wash a dish, clean a stove or floor, dress properly, eat properly. It was oppressive to me as a child.

When my mother retired at age seventy-five, she had become laissez-faire. I assumed it was because of age and loss of energy. I was not troubled.

But there were hints something was wrong. She had made a couple of tablecloths for my dining room, one for meat and one for dairy. For months, she sowed cross-stitch patterns of Hebrew letters for "Shabbat and Yom Tov," as well as images of candlesticks, challah, a wine decanter, a Kiddush cup, and pomegranates. Blue thread for the *milchig* one, blue and gold for *fleishig*. Three months after she gave us the tablecloths, she asked what else she could do, that would fill her time. "You could make us another tablecloth, but this one should be round and without Hebrew lettering." "Oh," she murmured in disbelief, "Did the others have Hebrew words on them?"

My mother slipped into dementia at a glacial pace. Looking back, I realize the first signs appeared in her early seventies. She died at ninety-three, as people often do from Alzheimer's, when she aspirated food and caught pneumonia. Otherwise she was in perfectly good health.

In the middle stage of the disease, her eyes would fill with fear and she would ask plaintively, "Bobbi, what's happening to me?" I'd pull her close, "Mommy, it doesn't matter. I will take care of you." Then she would relax in my arms, forgetting whatever thoughts had terrified her moments before.

I lived in a city more than two hours away. I considered moving my mother to Philadelphia, but I recognized that she was holding on to who she had been, because she knew every inch of the apartment where she'd lived since 1957, when I was seven years old. Widowed at age fifty-eight, she had already lived alone for many years. She had her systems, and everything had its place. She had cleaned, polished, scrubbed, dusted, and vacuumed this home for decades. The familiar space, its walls, shadows, and outlines, and the familiar objects within it, formed an exoskeleton that held her together as she slowly came undone from the inside.

~

My mother was the child of Jewish refugees from Poland and Russia who came to the United States during the mass migration of Jews in the late

Part I: Caring

nineteenth and early twentieth centuries. My grandmother fled the state-sponsored massacres known as pogroms. She had lived in a small village in Poland, a shtetl, created by laws that segregated Jews into ghettos where they were helpless against anti-Semitic marauders and raids by Russian soldiers. My grandfather was a tailor who escaped after being forcibly conscripted into the czar's army. He met his nineteen-year-old bride-to-be as he trekked on foot from Russia to Poland, eventually passing through her shtetl in the Pale of Settlement. They married and fled as refugees to the USA on steerage class, leaving all family behind, arriving on Ellis Island in 1905. Between 1880 and 1924, hundreds of Jewish villages were burned by rampaging mobs of peasants and soldiers. Thousands were murdered. Three million Jews fled to the United States, until immigration was cut back severely in 1924.

My grandmother never learned to speak English. She stayed as close to home as possible, except when, out of necessity, she went door to door during the Depression, selling home cleaning products for the Fuller Brush Company, behind her husband's back, thinking it would have shamed him to have known. During her first decade in the *Goldene Medina*,[1] she lived through a personal trauma when her third child, a three-year-old boy, was run over by a trolley car. She had left her oldest child, an eight-year-old girl, to watch her two baby brothers, a five-year-old and a three-year-old, on a crowded Bronx street. Without the girl noticing, the toddler had darted into oncoming traffic. Unable to cope with their responsibility for leaving such a young child to babysit even younger ones, my grandparents blamed the eight-year-old schoolgirl.

My mother was born just a couple months after the baby boy's death.* For my grandparents, her birth was redemptive. But the tragedy of the toddler's premature death, laid at the feet of his young sister, Rose, cast a long shadow over subsequent generations.

My mother was born just a couple months after the baby boy's death

My mom was born a few years before her little brother. She had sketchy memories of her joy of holding her little brother, then seeing her brother lying in a tiny coffin in their family living

---

1. For many Jews who made the dangerous trip across the Atlantic Ocean a century ago, America was known as *die Goldene Medina*, the Golden Land, where all dreams would come true.

room. Mom did not remember anyone explaining to her that it was the custom in the 1920s for deceased loved ones to lie in repose at home. Nor did she remember anyone explaining to her that he had died or what death meant. She did not remember her brother's name. But she remembered a sadness in their home. A sadness she experienced again a couple years later when her grandmother was lying in a coffin in the family living room.
—Cari

As I was growing up, the story of the family tragedy was repeated over and over. After each telling, my mother would conclude: "My parents always called Rose, 'the clipper.' What could that mean?" This question hung over the family like an oracular mystery.

When my aunt was ninety-one years old, she was still asking me the question, as if finding the answer might make the suffering of her life comprehensible.

My aunt died. My mother died. The question remained.

One day, suddenly, my mind parted and I saw the answer. I was shocked. Until they were gone, my unconscious had protected me from knowing the answer and having to share it.

As a student of Jewish mysticism since graduate school, I knew well a creation story dramatically different from the one in Torah. It was the famous myth of sixteenth-century Jewish mystic Isaac Luria to explain why the world is a broken place, formed by a mixture of good and evil.

In the beginning, God filled the whole universe. To create the world, God contracted, clearing space for Creation, pouring God's great light into shells or vessels. But the light was so powerful, it shattered the vessels, and everything fell from its proper place. The world as we know it was formed by the mingling of shattered shards and sparks of light. The sparks are holy. The shards are the husks that obscure the light. It is the task of Jews to repair the world from this cosmic catastrophe, by lifting the sparks through mitzvot and acts of loving-kindness.

The Hebrew word for the shard is *kelippah*. In Yiddish slang, it would have sounded like "clipper."

~

In recent years we have greatly expanded our understanding of transgenerational trauma, of how it can be transmitted in families not only through myths and stories, through emotional distress, parental behavior, through

Part I: Caring

family interaction, but also through our genes. "What human beings cannot contain of their experience—what has been traumatically overwhelming, unbearable, unthinkable—falls out of social discourse, but very often onto and into the next generation as an affective sensitivity or a chaotic urgency."[2]

I never understood why my mother's love for me was so threaded with anxiety, hypervigilance, reactivity, rage, and the terror that something terrible was always about to happen to me. In the 1950s and 1960s, I grew up in a sleepy village on the Hudson River in New York. It was as safe as any place could be. Nevertheless, if I was twenty minutes late getting home, my mother was often on the verge of hysterical screaming: "Where have you been? What took you so long? *You can't do this to me!*" As a teenager, I was accused of being thoughtless, selfish, and reckless for putting her through so much stress. Her terror was my fault. When I was in graduate school, my mother called every weekend. If I wasn't in the apartment when she called, she interrogated my roommates. "Are you telling me the truth? She's dead and you're not telling me. I can tell there is something wrong and you're hiding it from me." My roommates did not know how to deal with her. When my mother could not account for my whereabouts, she had visions of me lying dead somewhere.

She lived with ghosts that crept up her nervous system,* filling her with waves of unspeakable dread about losing her beloved only child to some awful death. It was the trauma of generations pouring through my grandmother, into my mother's body, and then shot into my nervous system.* As trauma therapist and teacher of cultural somatics, Resmaa Menakem writes, "We've been trained to think of the past in terms of a written historical record. But events don't just get written down; they get recorded and passed down in human bodies."[3]

She lived with ghosts that crept up her nervous system

See the full quote from Avery Gordon in my chapter on page 100. "The ghost or the apparition is one form by which something lost, or barely visible, or seemingly not there to our supposedly

---

2. Fromm, *Lost in Transmission*, xvi.
3. Menakem, *My Grandmother's Hands*, 72.

well-trained eyes, makes itself known or apparent to us, in its own way, of course..."[4] —Su

---

It was the trauma of generations pouring through my grandmother, into my mother's body, and then shot into my nervous system

I quote from Grace Cho:

> Trauma evacuates memory in that it perpetually disturbs one's sense of being settled. Memory is poised to take flight whenever it is threatened, when there is a sense of a trauma returning or of a new trauma that is about to happen. This sense of impending catastrophe is an illusion, however, because the trauma never quite arrives. It never arrives because it has already happened; it is already in the present as an effect of some persistent past. The traumatized subject is continually uprooted. She might seem to be in a familiar place, in the sense that she has been there before, and she will most likely return there again and again through the force of repetition. Yet this place is neither an origin nor a final destination, keeping her suspended between a failed remembering and an incomplete forgetting.[5]

See p. 100 in my chapter. —Su

My mother's anxiety persisted until she got dementia, when the most difficult parts of her personality were wiped away by the disease.* When my mother was in the early stages of Alzheimer's, we had a remarkable exchange. As I washed the dishes, she sat at the kitchen table calmly, so pleased just to be together. It suddenly struck me that my mother had lost her critical and anxious edge. I looked intently into her eyes.

"Mom, you are a lot easier to be with these days. You don't worry about anything anymore."

"Bobbi," she said, looking at me wide-eyed and incredulous, "I, I can't remember what to worry about!" We both laughed, until we cried.

---

4. Gordon, *Ghostly Matters*, 8.
5. Cho, *Haunting the Korean Diaspora*, 79.

Part I: Caring

the most difficult parts of her personality were wiped away by the disease

Ironically, one of the blessings of my mother's Alzheimer's was her forgetting. As my mother's Alzheimer's progressed, she forgot the layers of oppression and suffering she experienced through her whole life. As a result, an unknown side of my mother emerged. The mother I had known was a serious church woman with clear ethical principles that guided her life. She taught us to do the same. She only listened to hymns and sermons in the car or in the house when she was cooking. She would sing loudly, and most often off-key, with the hymns blaring from her cassette player as her prayer and devotion. She carried herself as a noble, gentle, proper lady. There was no space for frivolity or having fun just for the sake of having fun. The joyous, the spontaneous, and the fun-loving mother, no longer useful during times of war and dislocation, was replaced by the serious, goal-driven, striving-against-all-odds mother. Through her Alzheimer's, however, this survival strategy, which had long lost its effectiveness, was finally relinquished. These correct-behavior inhibitions left her. She came to love all kinds of music—pop songs, Korean folk songs, with beats to move her body, especially her hips, to dance. She would just get up from her seat, clap her hands, swing her hips, to the left, and to the right, to dance to the inexorable pull of the music. My mother became happy and carefree. She savored the moments with delicious food and good music. In the comforting haze of forgetting, I was able to re/acquaint myself to my mother, perhaps to her more true and authentic self. —Su

Because the troubling layers of her personality vanished first, I realized that my mother's anxious, critical, compulsive nature was not the core of who she was, as I had always thought. The rage, terror, and rigidity were caused by historical and intergenerational trauma, and the disease somehow wiped those memories away. "After months and years, unhealed trauma can appear to be a part of someone's personality."[6]

∼

After the big blizzard, my mother was not ready to let caregivers into her home, but she could not shop or prepare food. So once every couple weeks, I drove to New York to stay overnight, shop, cook, and freeze food, stock her up with groceries and fresh produce. But when I returned, the kitchen

---

6. Menakem, *My Grandmother's Hands*, 39.

would be cluttered with empty cans, wrappers, paper, cartons, jars, and packaging strewn all around. My trips were spaced too far apart, but I could not come more often. My life had become more complicated. Transgenerational trauma cast a long, mysterious shadow.

One of my first cousins had been murdered. She had been a poet and gifted pianist who took too much LSD in the '60s while living in the Village and Haight Ashbury, and who suffered with schizophrenia. She was the single mother of two daughters, and there were no other parents able to care for her children. My cousin was Rose's child, the one who had been the eight-year-old babysitter of the three-year-old run over by the trolley. Now it was Rose's child who had been killed.

My mother was the cherished youngest child who brought hope into what must have been a bleak and desolate home shattered by trauma and guilt. I was *her* daughter. In a moment of clarity, I saw the blueprint of my life and knew that one of the reasons I had been put on this earth was to love and continue to raise my cousin's children.

My husband and I took her two daughters, aged seven and thirteen, into our home with plans to adopt them. I continued the trips to my mother, sometimes taking my younger daughter with me. But a year later, my husband died suddenly while we were on vacation. I became a young widow at age forty-six, working full-time, with two traumatized children, and I could not take care of my mother by myself. I had to hire caregivers to live with her.

Two Jamaican women, Hyacinth and Oneill, helped me sustain my life. They were both attentive and skillful, but Hyacinth was kind and loving beyond measure. She was religiously devout and considered my mother to be a gift from God. When I hired her, she told me she had been desperate for work. Praying aloud in her car, she asked God to send her work so she could support her father in Jamaica and her daughter in the States. The next day she got a call from the elder care manager who was looking for caregivers for my mom. Hyacinth thought that God had answered her prayers. It turned out that Hyacinth was an answer to mine.

Hyacinth and I formed a very interdependent relationship over the years. I trusted her because I saw how tenderly she cared for my mother. Not only did she make sure she was clean, safe, and well-nourished. She was a companion. She took my mother with her when she shopped or traveled around the neighborhood; she talked with her, hugged and massaged her. She polished her nails, cut and styled her hair. She kept her physically strong and healthy for many years. Most of all, she loved her.

As my mother slipped deeper into dementia, the words she spoke most often were, "I love you." Long after her rational mind and most language evaporated, her emotional mind stayed intact and intuitive. She could sense who was kind and would declare, "I love you." When I visited, she would say it over and again: "I love you." Pause. "Have I told you recently? I love you." I could see the waves of affection repeatedly sweep across her face,* though she could not remember what she had said moments before.

I could see the waves of affection repeatedly sweep across her face

I remember my mother as someone who did not openly express her emotions. She laughed out loud only when she was with her sisters. I rarely saw her cry in public, but I suspect she did so privately in the bathroom or if she was outside alone somewhere. It did not occur to me that she was holding her emotions in as a measure of security.

Bobbi's reference to her mother saying "I love you" over and over again reminded me that Mom's common phrase was "that I love you goes without saying." As I grew older, I wondered why she did not outwardly express her joy or her tears, or even verbalize her love. I finally asked her why she always said that. I went on to tell her that I wanted to hear "I love you" coming from her mouth. At first, she didn't see the point, because of course she loved me/us. Why should she always have to say it? As she grew older, it became commonplace to hear "I love you" at the end of our times together, to which she added "Be careful." Bobbi's mother and mine had different end-of-life circumstances, but I am sincerely grateful to have heard the words "I love you" regularly, just as I believe Bobbi did. —Linda

---

When my mother attended my younger daughter's bat mitzvah in Philadelphia, a dear friend of mine came to wish her a congratulations. "Mazel tov, Mary! You must be very proud." My mother looked into her eyes, "I love you." My friend, a rabbi and spiritual teacher, exclaimed, "Bobbi, your mother is a guru! What everybody wants is for someone to look them deeply in the eyes and tell them they are loved. That's what your mother does all day long!"

This Old Woman . . .

This Old Woman Is Not What You Think

> Isn't my mother, is not
> what I thnk.
> She's a spiritual master
> trying to teach me
> how to carry my soul lightly
> how to make each step
> an important journey,
> every motion and breath
> anywhere
> as though anywhere
> were the center of the earth.[7]

Perhaps my mother could descend gently into oblivion because she felt safely held in love. She was daily in Hyacinth's tender care, and she trusted me to do what was best for her. Perhaps it was good luck. Perhaps it was because of which neural pathways were affected by the Alzheimer's plaques. Whatever the cause of my mother's remarkable good humor, I was filled with gratitude and was deeply dependent on Hyacinth to make my life possible.

Without Hyacinth, I would have had to uproot my family and overturn my life, my career, and the lives of my children. Because of Hyacinth, I could keep my mother in New York and visit her regularly rather than move her to Philadelphia. My mother had saved enough money for me to pay Hyacinth what she asked for. And when my mother's money began to run out and I had to stretch to pay her salary, I could do so. I knew Hyacinth's salary supported her family in Jamaica and in the States. It was important to me that Hyacinth's life worked for her as she was enabling my life to work for me. At times, Hyacinth had to babysit her grandson and would bring him to stay over at my mother's apartment. At times she took my mother back to her apartment in the Bronx.

She understood what it meant that I had adopted my cousin's children after their mother's murder. We were both working women and single mothers with the responsibility of two generations on our shoulders. We knew we could not have made our lives work as well as they did if not for each other. Our lives were not intimately intertwined. I lived in my world. She lived in hers. They were different worlds. But in the spheres where we touched, we were intertwined. Eventually I supported Hyacinth as she became a citizen of the United States.

---

7. Sholl, "This Old Woman . . . ," in Olson, ed., *Mother to Daughter*, 245.

Part I: Caring

∼

When Hyacinth accompanied my mother to Philadelphia for my younger daughter's bat mitzvah, I gave her my bedroom so that she could sleep near my mother and have a private bathroom. I slept on the couch in the living room and my daughters were in their bedrooms. Hyacinth could not believe I had given her my room and my bed. That is what I overheard her telling a friend on the phone. "Bobbi put me in her bed. My boss put me in her *own* bed!"

I had never heard Hyacinth refer to me as her boss before. Though she said this with delight, it marked the power difference between us. Hyacinth and I had thoughtfully, ethically, and carefully navigated the class and power differences between us through the years. She by caring for my mother with such dependability and tenderness; I by regularly expressing my deep gratefulness to her, paying her well for her work, and trusting the choices she made to care for my mother and her own family, balancing everyone's needs.[8] When she needed money for a new car, I loaned it to her like a friend, and she paid me back like a friend, fully and with appreciation. I was glad she'd known she could ask.

∼

In the years when I was responsible for my mother's care, I was very aware of the economic, class, and racial privileges which had enabled my mother and father, a secretary and a liquor salesman without college educations, to have purchased a co-op apartment in postwar America, to have saved and invested enough money so she/we could afford to hire caregivers for so many years. I was aware of the privilege that enabled me to get a fine education and to earn a good-enough living so I could take over when my mother's money ran out. Without those financial resources, the need to care for my mother for seventeen years could have been devastating. So much of what is said or written about Alzheimer's is the tragic loss of self

---

8. Ai-Jen Poo, in her book *The Age of Dignity: Preparing for the Elder Boom in a Changing America* makes a case that in order to care for the aging majority with dignity, we need to create and support domestic and home care workers to work and live with dignity. Domestic and home care workers are the fastest growing workforce due to the "silver tsunami" of aging population boom. See also, https://caringacross.org/building-caring-majority/.

and cognitive function. Or the enormous strain—emotional, physical, and financial—of having to care for a parent with the disease. That is all true.

But much less is written about the healing that can happen between family members when caring for someone with dementia. Dayle Friedman's beautiful article "Seeking the *Tzelem*: Making Sense of Dementia" is an important exception, as she shares vignettes of people with dementia and their familial and professional caregivers, and explores the meaning of dementia within a Jewish theological context. "Dementia . . . strips souls down to their essence. One daughter who flies across the country every few weeks to care for her father, a man with advanced dementia, says it is not a burden but a privilege. 'He's just pure *ḥesed* (loving-kindness),' she says, 'That's all that's left.'"[9] I heard from a friend that his mother lit Shabbos candles every day because she could not remember what day it was and thought everyday was Shabbat.

One of the most important things I learned in the years of my mother's illness was that people with dementia can still play important roles in relationships.* I sometimes express this by saying that the *neshama*, the soul, can still accomplish things in this world, even when the thinking mind is gone.

---

people with dementia can still play important roles in relationships

There is a famous midrash (rabbinic commentary) which says that the broken tablets of the Ten Commandments Moses smashed when he came down from Mount Sinai and saw the golden calf, and the whole tablets he received when he went up the mountain a second time, were both placed in the Ark of the Covenant the Israelites carried for the rest of their journey through the desert (Bava Batra 14b).

In the Talmud, this midrash is called upon to teach that an elderly scholar who has forgotten all his learning due to old age or disease, like the broken tablets, must be honored as if he still had all his cognitive abilities.

Rav Avraham Isaac Kook (1865–1935) renowned rabbinic scholar and Kabbalist went further in his teaching about the necessity to honor the elderly with dementia. He taught that within a person who has acquired knowledge from good deeds done throughout his life, even those that took place in the distant past, a residue of righteousness will always remain in his soul. This

---

9. Friedman, "Seeking the *Tzelem*."

Part I: Caring

residue, the aura of holiness and goodness, continues, regardless of the ravages of time and circumstance, and therefore ongoing reverence is necessary.[10] —Bobbi

When I walked into my mother's view, whether it was moments or weeks since the last time she saw me, her eyes would light up and she'd say, "I love you." It always felt as though a rare and precious bird had landed on my shoulder. As long as my mother's eyes lit up at the sight of me, the mother I most needed was still in there. I knew that she would eventually forget my name. But I believed she would never forget who I was. And I was right. When she could not remember what name to call me, I knew she recognized me by the light in her eyes.

My mother was an active participant in creating the circle of love between herself, Hyacinth, and me. That love kept all of us going for more than a decade, all single women carrying heavy burdens. It helped to sustain my mother, me, my daughters, Hyacinth, her daughter and grandchildren in the States, and Hyacinth's father in Jamaica.

∽

Six months before my mother died, in the winter, I was coughing up blood and had severe lower-back pain. I was tested for pneumonia and a kidney infection and was diagnosed with pneumonia.

When I got home from the hospital two days later, Hyacinth called to tell me my mother had been hospitalized with pneumonia and a urinary infection. A couple weeks later, I sat on her hospital bed slowly feeding her spoonfuls of a weighted sweet, milky white substance. Looking into her eyes, she met my gaze. I thought, "This is how I came into the world. This is how I am going to escort you out."*

This is how I am going to escort you out

Bobbi's and my mother both died in their early nineties. Their last days were somewhat similar in that bodily functions were limited. When my mother could not eat because of her hiatal hernia, the only thing possible was creamy white substances filled with nutritional boosters. As Mom's strength weakened, we began to offer a spoonful at a time, which she received

---

10. See Bieler, "Parshat Ki Tissa."

with a similar gaze. In my chapter, I wrote that one of the "holiest moments was to usher the one who gave me life, out of her life." —Linda

∽

While I was writing this piece, I picked up the phone and called Hyacinth. Was I looking at things through rose-colored glasses years later? Was I exaggerating the power of the love and healing that we had shared?

Hyacinth answered the phone right away, saying she had picked it up immediately when she saw my name on the screen and exclaimed, "Bobbi! We just got home from church. I was calling your name the other day! They say when you hear ringing, it means someone is calling your name. Have your ears been ringing?"

We caught each other up on our lives, her children and grandchildren, my children and grandchildren. I told her I was writing an article about my mother during the last years of her life and that I could not write about Mary without writing about her also. We were both tearful on the phone. Toward the end of our conversation, I said,

"Hyacinth, I miss you. I am going to drive up to Coop Village, in the Bronx, to see you."

I paused.

"I want to go to church with you."

"That would be special."

"What time is church?"

"It starts at 10 a.m., but I like to leave at 9 a.m."

"Oh, that's so early! I'd have to leave Philly too early to get to the Bronx by that hour! Maybe, I'll come in the afternoon, but then I'd miss church."

"You'll stay overnight."

"Oh, you have room for me in your apartment?"

"I'll give you my bed," she said.

QUESTIONS FOR REFLECTION

1. What unexpected emotional or spiritual gifts have you received while caring for another person?
2. How has historical or intergenerational trauma or resilience shaped your life and been passed down through body, story, and spirit?

PART I: CARING

3. How have you navigated the complexities of relationships with professional caregivers, especially those relationships characterized by differences of class, race, and power?

2

Stretching without Breaking

KATHLEEN T. TALVACCHIA

As I sit down to write this piece, over forty years since my mother's death at age fifty-seven from kidney disease, I am thinking about my young self,[1] who, along with my siblings and my father, experienced my mother's extended illness, dialysis treatments, and slow decline over the seven years leading up to her death—an experience for which none of us was really prepared. Negotiating the traumas and blessings of caretaking was something that my tween and teen self often found overwhelming, frightening, and confusing. Resources to help families in this situation were not so present in the 1970s, or if they did exist were not something that was present in our world. I am thinking particularly about how difficult it was for my young self, forced by circumstances to be older before I was wiser, to manage the issue of the boundaries between my mother's illness and my own life. The lines often blurred between her care and my own self-care, and in the necessary prioritizing of her needs, mine often got lost or were entirely absent. In that time my spirit wrestled to understand something that I did not realize was a deep struggle of the soul: What was required of me for her care? Because of the love I felt for my mother, what did I require of myself?

---

1. I was twelve when my mother got seriously ill, fourteen when she started dialysis treatments, and nineteen when she died.

Part I: Caring

What was required of me for my own self-care? How could I manage that inevitable conflict? And where was God in this mess?

The problem is not unique to me, of course, nor this situation; it insinuates itself into the very human conflicts related to care for the people we love over a lifetime. The relationships of care to which we commit ourselves—for example, to parents, children, life partners, siblings, dear friends—bump up against the inexorable conflict between care for the other in need and our self-care. In many ways the tension is fundamental to the experience of caretaking, a challenge of stretching toward the other without breaking ourselves apart.

I am one of the younger of the six children in our family, with an age difference of thirteen years between the oldest and youngest. It is no exaggeration to say that my mother had always been the emotional and practical glue* that held together this active and intense group of siblings. At the time of her illness, three of my older siblings were away, either living at school or working professionally, and for a large portion of those years my father commuted to a job that was out of the area and necessitated his living away from us for long periods of time. We all supported Mom's care as much as we were able, but much of the daily work of caretaking was the responsibility of the three youngest of us who lived at home. Additionally, my grandmother, an Italian immigrant with an extremely difficult personality, lived with us and required care. Her often destructive presence created an enormous amount of stress in the family system. For all of us there were enormous logistical and emotional struggles with which to cope; needing to comprehend the inevitable loss of the person who seemed to hold all of us together made it even more overwhelming.

> **emotional and practical glue**
>
> I am the youngest in a sibling group of four strong-minded people. Mom had distinct relationships with each of us, but she also had a way of holding us together. She was our emotional glue. I suspect that she worried about how we would stay connected to each other without her. As we have grown older, we do remain connected, albeit loosely since we no longer need to negotiate common decisions affecting our parents. We live very separate lives. —Linda

As a young girl dealing with this ongoing crisis, I felt the demands that stretched me in the extreme as I tried my best to respond. I was amazed when I came to understand the reality of God's grace that supported me toward strength that I did not know I possessed at all, let alone at a young age. In truth, I grew and matured from the struggles—eventually. But the other truth is just as real: I often profoundly struggled not to break apart, unable to find that balance. I count it as more abundant grace that I began to learn to develop a better sense of perspective and self-care over many years of maturity, therapy, and spiritual counseling.

Looking back, I realize that it would have been helpful to know then what I came to know much later about coping with caretaking. At that time I felt tremendous frustration and anxiety that I did not have any practical ways to understand how to care for my mother and how to care for myself. I was so deeply enmeshed in her care that I have worked hard as an adult to find some space between my mother's experience of her illness and my own experience of caring for her. Writing this reflection has provided needed emotional space and has helped me to offer my young self, in a spirit of compassion and empathy, some level of perspective about what it means to care for another while making sure to care for yourself.

In what follows I reflect personally upon some of the inherent and consistent conflicts I have come to understand between the obligations of caring for those we love who are in need and the boundaries of appropriate role, responsibility, and self-care. Each reflection seeks to articulate a different aspect of the ways that I came to understand the balance between caretaking for another and for myself. What are these ways? Through the wisdom gained from maturity, reflection, therapy, spiritual direction, and the study of theology, I came to understand four insights useful for support as we seek to maintain balance: (1) understanding the distinction between care and cure, (2) engaging the practices of listening well and cultivating compassion, (3) using resources from religious traditions and cultures, and (4) making a commitment to the hard work of seeking to maintain balance.

I offer these reflections as meditations that I hope will have something to say, not only to my young self, but to the young self in all of us who, as we care for those we love, seeks to understand more clearly how to stretch and not break.

CARE, CURE, AND STRETCHING WITHOUT BREAKING

The concepts of boundaries and obligations are formal categories of study in psychology, ethics, and law; however, for these reflections I look toward the everydayness of the caretaking work that we do in our personal lives in order to consider its presence in the energies of our spirit. I want to reflect practically on the spiritual issues of boundaries and obligations and, therefore, to understand the energy of soul* that connects us to the Divine, to the one who needs our care, to ourselves, and to the larger community as we engage in the practical issues of caretaking.

the energy of soul

When my mother became seriously ill, my father was incredibly devoted to my mother's medical care while also trying to care for the practical needs of me and my two sisters, who were all teenagers at the time. We never, however, talked about emotional/spiritual care of her or any of us. In terms of caring for the "soul," growing up in a particular Catholic frame, acts were always outwardly focused and relied on the authority of the Church. One attended Mass and lit a candle for a sick relative, and one would pay the church to have a prayer spoken for the ill or to participate in a novena. If someone was close to death, then one would bring in a priest to offer a standard prayer at the loved one's bedside. When thinking about our ability as family members to "cure the body or soul," we felt we had little power over what might happen. Power and control were left in the hands of authority, whether it be God or the doctors. Praying for God to intercede was your only option.

When I came to Buddhism, the theological focus moved from an external authority to oneself. There is no equivalent in Buddhism for the notion of soul. There is no place where one can locate a solid, unchanging anything, no less an eternal soul. Similar to Moore's view of soul as a quality of being, in Buddhism, our ability to be present and therefore offer healing care is intimately related to the state of one's own body, mind, and heart. As Buddhists, we cultivate compassion and wisdom to allow us to deeply be with things as they are, unburdened by personal preferences and therefore open to what might be most skillful in a given moment.

This theological perspective doesn't offer me the comfort of a belief in an afterlife or a God but does land me in a sense of mystery and a deep lived faith in the healing potential of love and wisdom. —Laura

I have found Thomas Moore's classic work *Care of the Soul* to be a helpful resource in thinking about a way to understand the spiritual issues present in the conflict between boundaries and obligations. In his work as a psychotherapist, Moore finds it important to understand the symptoms that people bring into their therapeutic relationship as the voice of their soul speaking in their life. He advocates a focus on "care of the soul," which is "a continuous process that concerns itself not so much with 'fixing' a central flaw as with attending to the small details of everyday life, as well as to major decisions and changes."[2] While not using the word in the context of explicit religious belief, for him soul, rather than a concrete object, is "a quality or a dimension of experiencing life and ourselves. It has to do with depth, value, relatedness, heart, and personal substance."[3] His focus on soul care allows him to radically rethink the role of care in relation to the task of cure that he understood to be his role as a therapist. Specifically, he sees a distinction between care of the soul and cure of the soul. The action of caring engages a spiritual process of seeing the stirrings of the sacred in everyday life. The action of curing is a therapeutic process of seeking to fix a problem. He states, "A major distinction between care and cure is that cure implies the end of trouble. If you are cured, you don't have to worry about what was bothering you any longer. But care has a sense of ongoing attention."[4] Thus, rather than a focus on an intervention that produces a change on a more superficial level, he advocates for psychology to focus on an ongoing care of soul in which substantive human transformation can be effected over time.

I like Moore's distinction between care and cure.* It provides insight into my thinking about the spiritual tensions that exist in the everyday living of the conflicts between boundaries and obligations. It provides a way to put the caretaking conflict in a meaningful spiritual context. Caretaking of someone who is chronically ill involves negotiating the tension of being present to them in their illness while at the same time participating in activities that are part of their comfort and cure. The conflict of boundaries occurs because inevitably the lines between care and cure become blurred. A major aspect of a caretaking relationship involves not just our active presence but our active participation in many aspects of what needs to be done therapeutically—aspects that are more properly in the category of cure. They cannot help but become indistinct over time.

---

2. Moore, *Care of the Soul*, 3–4.
3. Moore, *Care of the Soul*, 5.
4. Moore, *Care of the Soul*, 18–19.

PART I: CARING

Moore's distinction between care and cure

Kathy's reference to understanding the distinction between care and cure spoke volumes to me. When my mom was recovering from her open-heart surgery, I didn't agree with the siblings' insistence that she get up and walk around so she could get better. When Mom refused to get out of bed and didn't want to eat, I defended her choice. Maybe it was because I was practicing the "art" of pastoral care, or maybe it was because I am the youngest of the siblings, or maybe it was because my instinct is to care before cure. Perhaps it was all three.

Interestingly, years later when Mom was recovering from her hip surgery and her overall health was deteriorating rapidly, I wanted her to eat so she could be cured. I realize now that she was much closer to death, so I pushed her to do everything possible to stop that from happening.

Two of my siblings have suffered strokes in the last two years, and as I now reflect on my first instinct at their bedside, caring was my first response. Both were fortunate enough to receive the life-saving procedure that released the blood clots. The miracles of modern medicine took care of the cure. However, I cannot predict what will happen if I ever have to be a caregiver for any of my three siblings. As I have matured in my understanding of pastoral care, I recognize and lean into my basic instinct of care before cure. —Linda

When we care for someone who is ill, we walk a journey with them and are present to them in that suffering. But we also have specific tasks that participate in their comfort, which helps them to function in their environment, such as bathing them, advocating with insurance companies, taking them to doctors' appointments, helping with medicines, and taking care of a household. The emotional and spiritual tasks of care are intense and demanding in themselves, but we can often get overwhelmed by the simultaneous and corresponding demands of participating in activities of comfort and cure, which are frequently constant. Sometimes the tasks of cure require some level of expertise for which we have little experience but must perform anyway. The spiritual (as well as practical) challenge becomes finding a way to balance the demands of care and cure as much as possible.

Stating the conflict in this way helps me to understand better where to locate the necessary boundaries of self-care that we need, and the relationship of those boundaries to the obligations that are morally part of our actions. It places the work of caretaking within the cocoon of God's care for the person in need and for us. When we look at boundaries as part of "care for the soul" we can begin to see the presence of the sacred in the experience that can provide perspective for our obligations.

How might this be pertinent in our everyday activities of caretaking? Knowing that our responsibility is to care rather than cure* can help us to be more present to the person for whom we care. In order to maintain that presence over the length of the illness, we have a responsibility to ourselves and to the other person to take the time we need for self-renewal. In this way we can continue to be present to the person in their illness and engage in whatever logistics and activities are needed that are part of maintaining their welfare. Knowing that we participate in the activities of cure but are not responsible *to be* the cure can help us to sustain the activities of care. Our task, then, is to support that which can cure, but we are primarily responsible to help make an environment where both care and cure can happen most effectively.

---

our responsibility is to care rather than cure

Thanks for this reminder, Kathy. My impulse is to pray for cure. It is much harder for me to give care long-term when cure or healing does not look likely, because of the pain I feel.

There are numerous stories of Jesus healing individuals physically, mentally, and spiritually. Often the declaration from Jesus accompanying these healings is "your faith has made you whole." What does it mean when someone's illness or impairment is not cured, not healed? Does it suggest that they, or those praying for them, have not had enough faith? Growing up I was taught that the "effectual fervent prayer of the righteous avails much" (cf. Jas 5:16 KJV). That is, if anyone who is living a righteous life prays, without doubting, their prayers will be answered.

Twenty-four years before Mom died, I prayed for Dad to be cured from cancer. As his condition worsened, I wondered if I were living righteously enough for my prayers to be "effectual." One day it dawned on me to ask myself, "What does Dad want? What if my prayers run contrary to what he wants for his life? What if this is his time to die?" Then, I began praying for Dad's wholeness as I realized Jesus said, "Your faith has made you whole," not your faith has cured you. My prayer journey with my dad prepared me for what and how to pray twenty-plus years later when I journeyed with my mom. —Cari

Part I: Caring

This wisdom—that we are responsible to participate in the actions of cure and to know that our presence of care is our primary responsibility—would have provided some perspective in my efforts to care for my mother. In my youth and inexperience, I often engaged in a type of magical thinking (born, I'm sure, from fear and panic), believing on some level of which I was not fully conscious that if I cared for my mother with complete vigor and total commitment, she would not die. This often clouded my own capacity to care for myself, which tilted my coping mechanisms away from stretching and towards breaking. Practically, this meant that I would work myself to exhaustion attempting to take care of my mother's needs, take care of household responsibilities, keep up with my studies, and try to have some semblance of a high school life.

While magical thinking seems not an unusual thought when caring for a loved one, understanding it as a young person is extremely difficult. Here, then, is the first lesson that I came to understand: The demands of engaging in care and participating in cure can stretch us beyond what we imagined we could handle, but we stretch without breaking when we look to find some level of balance between the two. In order to cope with the stress of the stretching that is required, it helps to ground that stretching in an understanding that our responsibility first and foremost is to care and be present while participating in activities of cure as needed.

SOME PRACTICES OF STRETCHING WITHOUT BREAKING

When we reflect upon what we owe those we love in their need, and what we owe ourselves in our own need, it may feel like a truism to say, simply, that both must be done. While this is substantially true, therein lies the main conflict in our action as well as in our spirit: it is easier to say you have to do both than to actually be able do both consistently. Inevitably the two are in tension because it is almost always a conflict of two competing goods. The challenge, then, becomes developing ways to live positively through and with these tensions *in real time*.

This often seemed like an impossible task for me as a young person, and one that I have come to understand is a common experience of the human condition. It is exactly in this place, though, in the messy and conflicting actions of the spiritual everydayness of caretaking, that we begin to find some steadiness.

The second insight that I offer to my young self are two spiritual practices—learned over many years both in the activity of the moment and in the quiet of contemplation—that have helped me to maintain a better balance: learning to listen well and cultivating compassion. When I was caring for my mother I had to learn quickly to listen to what she said she needed—for example, help going to the bathroom, someone to bring her medication, or assistance going to the doctor—but it was difficult to understand the needs that were not so concrete or clearly stated, especially if they were emotional needs.

I see now that sometimes she herself did not even know what she needed, either physically or emotionally. And for that matter, neither did I. When I could not comprehend her need, I felt inadequate. A sense of compassion—both for myself in my lack of comprehension and for her emotional frustration and fears as she faced her increasing limitations—would have helped me to be more resilient rather than being angry at myself.

Learning to listen well is the first practice that helps maintain the balance of caretaking and self-care. It might be the single most important practice that builds the capacity to stretch without breaking. Yet it is so challenging to live out!

I often find it difficult to avoid being overtaken by the complex feelings involved in caring for someone I love who is in need. It seems a common human experience that love, fear, resentment, blessing, hope, and grief can blur together in an empathetic stew. Understanding that this is a common issue of caretaking is a relief in some ways but nonetheless a challenge to sort out. As I have learned to listen more effectively—attentively and openly—to what another is saying, I find it easier to develop good boundaries. What is the suffering that the person is experiencing, and what is my own suffering? Asking myself this simple question keeps me grounded in the reality of separating my experience from the experience of the loved one who is suffering.

I learned that in order to hear well, the questions about suffering must be placed in the proper perspective of our lives as existing within social and interpersonal contexts related to justice and injustice. Suffering, whether it is another's or our own, needs to be heard as both an individual experience *and* as one that exists within an intersectional web of cultures, experiences of social bias and resistance, and engagements with power. Understanding the impact of the social locations of race, gender and sexuality, class, disability status, and religious affiliation (among other categories), which permeate our lived realties, is significant and necessary to learning to listen well. In a society in which social inequities impact and shape our experiences, the question that discerns the boundaries between our suffering and that of the person for whom we care must be placed within that critical understanding. We cannot learn to listen well without it.

Seeking to listen well helps me to get a better sense of what the person is asking of me in caretaking. I gain perspective that helps me maintain a stronger balance. I can maintain a steadier pace in the grueling long-distance run of caretaking, saving energies for what might be greater needs at another time. Additionally, I am more equipped to avoid the trap of unintentionally disempowering another. It helps me to keep an awareness right up front of the energies and competencies that they possess and of their need to remain in control of their lives while much in their context undermines their sense of control.

Listening well also means listening to myself with more empathy and awareness. I can hear my needs more clearly and put them into the negotiating mix of what I owe another and what I owe myself. Listening to myself with more empathy helps me to push back guilt and place my very human limitations in a compassionate context. I have learned better to respect my needs and give better care to them. Even in those inevitable moments when my own self-care must be put aside for a time, rather than repressing or ignoring my needs, I have learned that sometimes I need to put them on the shelf for a bit, as it were, and make a promise to myself to get to them as soon as possible.

The practice of listening well depends upon hearing the presence of God in the experience of caretaking. This was perhaps what I was least able to do as a young person. I both relied on God, in a supplicatory sort of way, and felt abandoned by God.* The feelings were confusing: I understood instinctively that I was only able to cope on some level with the situation because of God's grace, yet I could not understand why the illness had to happen at all, and moreover why God had let it happen without an intervention of cure. It was a long journey to get from that place to a new place of listening in faithful confidence for God's presence and support in the mysteries of human frailty. The simple answer is that I only began to listen well to God later in my life, when I was able to face the necessity of wrestling with God, and like Jacob, demanding a blessing (Gen 32:22–32).

abandoned by God

As a young child I felt God's presence in a deep, palpable sort of way. But in my teenage years, as I experienced depression, I felt abandoned by God. At some point I discovered Psalm 13 and it became my anthem. "How long, O LORD; will You ignore me forever? How long will You hide Your face from me?" (Ps 13:2 NJPS).

The Hebrew refrain, *Ad Ana*, translated here as "How long," reverberated in my soul. Ignored by God. Forgotten by God. For how long? In the darkness of the depression I felt trapped in an eternal wasteland, and allowing myself to articulate the yearning was all that I could do. The language of the psalm, the fact that it existed, comforted me because it so captured by own sense that God's face was hidden from me. "How long will You hide Your face from me?" In the periods of my great suffering I turned to God. The words of the tradition supported me in my crying out. While I didn't get any profound responses, the crying out was a lifeline for me. Eventually, it was that commitment to crying out that led me into chaplaincy, a place where so many people need permission and partners in the crying out.

As a chaplain I have integrated psalms into my pastoral practice regularly. One of my favorite psalms is Psalm 27. While Psalm 13 lives primarily in the torment, Psalm 27 begins: "The LORD is my light and my salvation; whom shall I fear? the LORD is the strength of my life; of whom shall I be afraid?" (Ps 27:1 KJV). This psalm conveys a confidence about the psalmist's relationship with God. The only way that I was able to come to this confidence was by blessing the cry and letting it be for as long as it remained. When I tried to control it or change it, I always failed. But when I surrounded myself with people who could embrace me in the anguish of the cry, the cry was slowly able to dissolve. And I could experience God as my light and my salvation, *ori vi'shi*. One of the things I love in this psalm is that even with the confidence of the beginning of the psalm, there's still an echo of Psalm 13 as the psalmist pleads: "Do not forsake me, do not abandon me, O God my deliverer. Though my father and mother abandon me, the LORD will take me in" (Ps 27:9–10 NJPS). Even with an affirmation of God who helps and saves, there's a reminder of the lurking anger, abandonment, and forsaking. The psalm is teaching that we don't need to hide the full spectrum of possibilities that exist in our relationship with the Divine.

And, finally, we return to mothers (and fathers). In verse 10 the psalmist says "Though my father and mother abandon me, the LORD will take me in." In my mind, the forsaking parents have simply died. It's possible that they have done something

> more than that. It's possible that they abandoned the psalmist with negligent or abusive or inept behavior. But even if they were exquisitely phenomenal parents, they still abandoned the psalmist at the time of their death, when they could no longer provide loving arms in this chaotic world. And that is the moment when God must "take [us] in." For some of us, the moment of our parents' death is a moment of God's abandonment too. And if we allow ourselves to cry out in that abandonment, perhaps we will eventually experience that cry as being heard. But it is also possible that in that moment of parental abandonment, the Divine's presence can hold us, and that is miraculous. —Mychal

Cultivating compassion is another practice that both builds resiliency to negotiate the challenge of caring for another and honors self-care. In fact, the meaning of *compassion*, "to suffer with," represents the inherent conflict: the desire to care for the suffering of others and the desire to protect our human need to step away from it. Spiritual writer Henri Nouwen states the conflict clearly:

> Compassion is hard because it requires the inner disposition to go with others to the place where they are weak, vulnerable, lonely, and broken. But this is not our spontaneous response to suffering. What we desire most is to do away with the suffering by fleeing from it or finding a quick cure for it.[5]

This is the reason compassion must be cultivated. While it is true that we must stretch toward greater compassion, we need to guard against the boundaries becoming fuzzy in the desire to be compassionate. The call to compassion, and the struggle to negotiate its tensions between suffering with another and losing ourselves, requires attentive awareness of the context of the person for whom we care and the context of our self-care. It requires the courage to look at human suffering in all of its complex social realities and not to look away. Cultivating compassion, thus, is an outgrowth of learning to listen well.

Learning to be compassionate to myself* amid the work of caretaking was the most significant spiritual and psychological learning for my own maturation. Once I could see clearly the cost to my well-being that my lack of compassion presented, I learned to listen to my needs better and to value them more fully. I came to understand the fact that care for others without care for yourself is spiritually hollow. Without compassion for myself I was like a tree with shallow roots, unable to act with the full measure of spiritual

---

5. Nouwen, *A Spirituality of Caregiving*, 19.

strength needed to weather a storm. It also does not work well in practice. I could not effectively act justly with my mother when I could not extend that same justice toward myself.

Learning to be compassionate to myself

"You've got to pace yourself because this is a marathon." That is what I told myself often as I was caregiving for my mom. I reminded myself that I needed to be healthy and happy to be more able to support her in the ways she deserved.

Self-compassion was often made harder by comments from others. Most of the times I visited Mom in Baltimore, I did not go to church with her since I worked in a church in New York City on Sundays. When I did attend church with her, most of the time she and I went to the new church she joined. One Sunday she and I decided to attend worship service at the church of my childhood. Immediately following the service, a family friend made a beeline to me to tell me I needed to spend more time with my mother. She warned me that if I didn't, I would regret it when my mother died.

So many thoughts and feelings flooded me at the same time. "Who are you to say this to me when you don't even know how much time and money I give to take care of my mom?" "Is she expecting the same from my brothers, and has she confronted them in the same way?" Followed by, "Maybe I am not spending enough time or doing enough."

I was still trying to determine what the balance should be for my self-care and my caregiving responsibilities. In a paradoxical way, the challenge of this family friend helped me come to peace about how I was living out my caregiving responsibilities. Her challenge to me pushed me to assess what I was actually doing for my mother separate from what others might perceive. Making this distinction was liberating for me. —Cari

The practices of learning to listen well and cultivating compassion point toward a fundamental goal: strengthening our capacity to love deeply and without reservation. It is in this work of love that we learn just how far we can humanly stretch in the care for a loved one without breaking. We enter into relationships of caregiving because of that love, understood in its most complex and mysterious meanings. Perhaps that love is based on a sense of duty or gratitude or forgiveness, or on abiding joy. In the last, our love, in whatever form it takes, grounds and fuels our capacity for taking care of someone to and with whom we are bound.

Part I: Caring

Virginia Stem Owens, speaking of her long years of caring for her mother, who had dementia, describes this phenomenon in a way that feels right to me. She believes that ultimately love is a choice we make. She states,

> Loving people is such a burden. If love, in and of itself, weren't the center from which life flows, if it didn't, as Dante says, move the stars, how could we bear such weight? Nevertheless, love is also all that endures. Like most of God's work, it is double-bladed. Its seed grafted into us, it may begin as an instinct, but in the end, love is a choice. As for free creatures, it must be. It is indistinguishable from choosing life.[6]

Thus, choosing to love and care for another is choosing life. If we want to live fully, then taking on the burdens and blessings of caretaking becomes an integrated part of our lives. We choose to love, both the person for whom we care and ourselves. This is the abiding lesson for me about practices that nurture the ability to stretch without breaking. In choosing life, despite that which we sometimes cannot bear, we are making a *commitment to struggle to find the balance* that sustains and holds us in its insatiable motion. Choosing to love, learning to listen well, and cultivating compassion provides resources that help us to navigate stretching without breaking.

RELIGIOUS AND CULTURAL RESOURCES FOR STRETCHING WITHOUT BREAKING

A third insight for my young self involves making full use of the religious and cultural resources that have influenced us and shaped the ways we relate to the world. The ideas, traditions, and beliefs that formed us culturally and as members of religious communities of believers are powerful influences (both positive and negative), as well as resources that we bring to the experience of finding a balance between boundaries and obligations. In this final reflection I want to consider some values from my cultural and religious tradition that influenced the work of caring for my mother.

As I reflect back, I see the centrality of my Roman Catholic Christian upbringing as a major influence that formed my response. I attended Catholic schools for the majority of my education and was profoundly formed in the tradition's emphasis on the presence of God in human experience, and our response to the grace of God's presence through our actions of

---

6. Owens, *Caring for Mother*, 163.

care in the world. The Catholic tradition refers to this as the principle of sacramentality. Theologian Thomas H. Groome describes this principle, explaining its emphasis on God's presence and human response in daily action: "The sacramental principle means that *God is present in humankind and we respond to God's grace through the ordinary and everyday of the life of the world.*" [7] Thus, God's spirit and human action work together for the care of the world and all that is in it. Relatedly, the Catholic tradition of moral education emphasizes the development of a living faith that does the work of justice in the world. It is a formation of character as well as the development of specific virtues that hold a person accountable to live out the justice of God in their personal lives and to challenge social injustice in the world. This powerful religious worldview combined with an explicit Italian cultural value, operating in my three-generation family of origin and the larger cultural Italian American community, that stressed the maintenance and protection of the family. All around me in my experiences were examples and images of large extended families caring for parents and elders.

The power of these two influences was undeniable, but they also had a shadow side that could be just as influential, and sometimes harder to see clearly enough in order to break away from it. Within a spirituality and morality that prioritized faith as expressed through works of mercy and care, at times I struggled with guilt for not being able to manage, or not wanting to engage, whatever needed doing. Within a cultural system that valued family care, I could not always find the space for my own care. Part of the psychological and spiritual healing that I had to do after my mother's death involved learning how to better respond to the negative effects of those shadow sides.

The resources of my ethnic culture and my religious tradition grounded my sense of who I was and how I approached the world. It taught me about the obligations of caretaking that helped me to stretch as far as I was able to care for my mother in her need, providing me resources that helped me to grapple with the demands of not breaking apart: justice to oneself, the reciprocity of care, and the presence of God's grace in the midst of the struggle. I was not always able to be effective in that struggle, but I have come to see their influence and embrace their wisdom more fully.

Engaging the resources of culture and spiritual and religious tradition helps us to see our struggle within a larger framework of meaning that helps us to make sense of experiences that seem to make no sense. This

---

7. Groome, *What Makes Us Catholic*, 84 (italics original).

wisdom supports our attempts to stretch without breaking, helping us to place those struggles within a lager construct of meaning and purpose.

STRETCHING WITHOUT BREAKING ON THE JOURNEY OF CARETAKING

Here is the final insight that I offer to myself as a conclusion: The journey toward an effective balance between boundaries and obligations begins with this commitment: that we work faithfully to find and maintain—and find again once it is lost—a sense of equilibrium in the inevitable struggle between care and cure. We make that commitment relying on practices that can help us sustain that balance, such as learning to listen well and cultivating compassion. Drawing on the resources of our cultural and spiritual traditions, we can construct a scaffolding to support and sustain the work of care from a spiritual center. We do this as a response to all that we feel obliged to give out of our duty and responsibility, but also, and maybe most importantly, from the love we feel, or hope to find, in the action of caretaking. Reminding ourselves to care for ourselves in the same measure that we care for those we love can provide the strength we need to sustain stretching without breaking.

QUESTIONS FOR REFLECTION

1. How old were you when you lost your mother? How old do you *feel* as you grieve her loss? In what ways are the two in dialogue?

2. In what ways has your religious or spiritual tradition been a resource to you in your grieving? Or a barrier?

3. What are some of the practices that help you to cope with the demands of stretching without breaking?

3

Caring for Babygirl

CARI JACKSON

JUST AS I WAS preparing to relocate from Washington, DC to New York City to attend seminary, my mother in Baltimore began presenting signs of dementia. As I was making the decision about what I should do, I reflected a lot about Mom's life journey.

More than a decade earlier, I had moved from New Jersey to Maryland in order to help care for my father as he was dealing with colon cancer. I felt blessed to play a major role in his care, have special moments with him, and provide support to my mother throughout his illness and subsequent death. Of course, I should do the same for Mom. But I struggled to know what I should do about my spiritual calling. How to care for Mom and myself.

Mom and Dad loved to worship together in our Pentecostal church. They were both very involved in church ministry. Dad taught adult Sunday school, organized activities for youth, formed and conducted a twenty-five-plus-piece orchestra, established and led a Boy Scout troop, and more. In addition to supporting Dad in all his endeavors, Mom's main gift to the church was her rich and robust mezzo-soprano voice that sounded much like opera singer Jessye Norman's. She sang in the choir and was a soloist in our church and in many places throughout Baltimore. Often Mom sang and Dad accompanied her on violin. They enjoyed being together. Their love and service together inspired many people.

After Dad's death, Mom said, "My song is gone." For a while, she was not able to sing because singing reminded her of the hole Dad's death left in her. Hearing the absence of him accompanying her on the violin intensified her grieving.

Gradually, she was able to sing again as her gift would not be silent. When Mom began singing again, it was in completely new contexts for her. First, she began to sing in the choir in the Episcopal church of a family friend. Then, in the Maryland Chapter James Cleveland Workshop Choir, a statewide community gospel choir. In this choir, she made lots of new friends, many of whom were the ages of her children and grandchildren. With my brother and sister-in-love, who were also in the choir, Mom traveled to and sang in communities across the country.

SHE CHOSE TO SING

(written in honor of Mom's seventy-fifth birthday)

> A motherless child
> scared and lonely
> feeling unwanted and unloved
> without a home, nowhere to go.
>
> A gift of three shiny pennies tell her
> of a father.
> Moving from pillar to post reminds her
> of a mother.
> The orphanage was her home.
>
> When it was time to entertain
> in the street for food and money,
> she tried to hide
> from the jeers of passersby.
> Yet to have a home
> she had to give a song.
>
> Through her tears,
> the little girl chose to sing.
>
> The first love song she heard
> told her of amazing grace.
> Then came an invitation

"Open your voice to Me and sing my song
for all the world to know my love."

Wanted, loved, and blessed by God,
the teenage girl chose to sing.

A "dear Christian friend"
asked her to love him, marry him,
walk life's journey together
and sing with him
'til death would part them.

Filled with the joy of being loved,
the young woman chose to sing.

As the years passed, she grew weary—
not enough money for too many needs.
Her love said to her
"Sing our song with me and
we will make it."

Through joy-filled years,
the wife and mother chose to sing.

After forty years, when the spirit of her love passed on
she felt scared and all alone,
having a house, yet without him,
not having a home.

Once again, a motherless child
feeling unloved and unwanted.
She believed the song that she had sung
was gone forever.

Yet her memories reminded her
of songs yet to be sung
to let others know that
they too are wanted,
they too are loved.

With her well-used voice,
the old woman chooses to sing.

    Mom had become a member of a Pentecostal church at age fifteen. Her aunt Josephine introduced her to a Pentecostal Apostolic church. There, she met God, and my Dad. Mom was a member of that congregation for thirty years. Because of a disruptive church schism, Mom and Dad joined another Pentecostal Apostolic congregation, where they remained for almost twenty years until Dad's death.

During the first thirty years, the pastor drilled into all the members that they were not to associate with those who were not "saved"—that is, baptized and living a holy life, according to Pentecostal Apostolic doctrine. Being saved was paramount to everything that guided Mom's life.

For Mom to become a member of a Baptist church after Dad's death was a bold and unconventional act, especially given that she had been steeped in Pentecostalism for fifty years. By this action, Mom claimed her spiritual authority as a child of God to carve out her salvation on her own terms. Once she did this, Mom expanded in many areas of her life. For example, this good Pentecostal woman who had been taught only to wear dark colors in order not to be too flashy was now wearing bright red and yellow most of the time. While she began wearing brighter colors when Dad was still alive, in her reinvention after his death, she went full throttle. She began painting her nails—something she had rebuked me about years before.

Mom claimed a more joyful and liberatory salvation. What helped her to claim this authority was her strong belief that all children of God (which for her was everybody) were of equal value. No longer did she direct her life based on every word spoken by ministers. She relied more on her own discernment and her own relationship with God to guide her life. And she embraced what was a new concept for her, that God wanted her to be happy.

Her newly embraced spiritual authority helped Mom be able to reframe her thoughts about my sexuality. I had known since age nine that my affectional and romantic attractions were to females. All my childhood crushes were for women and girls. I tried to hide this from my parents and the whole world because the Pentecostal church taught that homosexuality was a sin and an abomination. I was extremely angry at God that I was considered an abomination for something I did not decide for myself. My sexuality was as innate as my skin color.

When I "came out" to Mom,* she expressed that she and Dad had known about my sexuality for years. To my surprise, Mom named in correct chronological order every girl or woman I had been attracted to through the years. To my amazement, she said, "I know I've been taught homosexuality is wrong, but I see God all through your life. So, I will leave it all to God." This moment had only been made possible because of the spiritual authority Mom began claiming in her life.

When I "came out" to Mom

One of the burdens of losing my mother at a young age was the loss of engaging her as I was growing into an authentic sense of myself. I came to understand my queer identity a full six years after her death. I have often wondered how she would have reacted to it. My sense is that she would have negotiated her discomforts in a way that saw my life in its fullness and in her deep love. In the end, I think she would have had a similar reaction as Cari's mother did to her disclosure. Cari's story has provided a healing moment of reflection and resolution for me. —Kathy

As Mom experienced more joy in her relationship with God, she also allowed her humor to show. My brothers and I began saying to each other, "I didn't know Mom was so funny." Because Dad was a profoundly serious person, Mom had been sharing her humor in only small measure to be more matched with Dad. And because there was such strong emphasis in the Pentecostal church to be "sober-minded," it had been instilled in her that to be lighthearted was being frivolous and not fully recognizing all the suffering Jesus endured for her salvation. As Mom claimed a more joyful and liberatory salvation, our family and friends were blessed to have more times of laughter and adventure with her.

After several years of this reemerged Mom, dementia began presenting.

Throughout Mom's season of reinvention—and perhaps inspired by it—I began honoring my calling to ordained ministry. Just as I was finally following the spiritual calling to professional ministry I had resisted for two decades, it was becoming more and more apparent that Mom needed care. I was already accepted to Union Theological Seminary in New York City and was scheduled to move there. I was in a quandary as to what I should do. Pursuing professional ministry and caring for my mother felt like competing roles God would have me engage.

I prayed for clarity about what to do. I asked whether I should delay seminary for another several years, not attend seminary, or attend a seminary closer to Mom in Baltimore. The messages I received for a few years had been abundantly clear that I was to attend Union. But given what was happening with Mom now, I wondered if I had misunderstood what I had believed to be God's direction for my life. My ambivalence about what to do was exacerbated by the fact that my relationship with my mother had just finally become what I had longed for it to be for years.

Part I: Caring

Throughout my growing up, Mom had very specific expectations for what my life should look like. Because she had been placed in an orphanage* by her mother and never knew her father, family was extremely important to her. And especially her relationship with her daughter, her only daughter. Mom said to me often, "You are Momma's company." She was unwaveringly clear about the image she had in mind for what my companionship with her was to look like. It was to be the fulfillment of what she had longed as a young girl to have with her mother.

---

orphanage

Reading Cari's chapter brought something of my own life into focus. Like Cari's mom, my mom was placed in an orphanage as a child, though my mom only remained there for about three years before her parents were able to take her back into their home. (See p. 122 in Mychal's chapter.) Cari's writing has gotten me thinking about caring for the one who didn't receive care—for the one who organized her identity around giving care but didn't have role models for her caring, so her methods could feel rough around the edges. But she knew how to love. I think about this as my mother's legacy, a strong, passionate love that has made reconciliation possible. —Mychal

Mom had not known how to relate with me, fully seeing the person I was, distinct from her. She and I bumped heads often and both experienced lots of heartache in our relationship. When I was in my early thirties, Mom had disappointed me yet again when she decided not to come hear me sing a solo at the Washington National Cathedral. Because music was a strong thread that wove through the fabric of our family, in her pride, initially she said she would come. The day of the event, she told me she would not come. Her reason was that this event was an AIDS healing service and I was singing with my church choir from Metropolitan Community Church, a spiritual home for LGBTQ+ individuals. She believed her attendance at this worship service would be affirming what she had been taught was sin. Although she had resolved to leave my salvation and life to God, she still could not bring herself to affirm my sexuality.

In my heartbreak and anger, I shouted at God. "Why can't she love me and accept me just the way I am?" I heard the reply, "Love her and accept her just the way she is." This response from Spirit made me even angrier. Once I realized that accepting her was part of my spiritual journey, I began making small steps toward accepting her. To my amazement, this new way of relating with my mother transformed our relationship. As I simply loved her instead of judging her, she began to do the same. Finally, Mom and I were cocreating the honest, loving relationship we had both longed for for years.

After all the years of struggle, longing for the quality of the mother–daughter relationship I had wanted and needed, dementia was taking my mom away from me.

"Honor thy father and thy mother." This scriptural mandate was some of the spiritual breast milk from which I drank since my earliest memory. Even during my years of teenage rebellion and my twentysomething-year-old period of individuation, this mandate always tempered my actions. Now, I was faced with the question, How was God calling me to honor my mother in this season of her life and the season of my own life?

If my mother had been dealing with an illness that was not cognitively oriented, I would have talked with her about which direction I should take. But that was not the case. I could not rely on my mother's input as I needed to make a critical decision impacting her life and mine.

During this period of wrestling, one day I heard the words in my spirit, "I took care of Gladys before you were born." I asked, "God, is that you?" I was uncertain whether the words I heard were spoken to me by Spirit or if I had manufactured them myself as a way to find peace and be able to move forward with my seminary plans without guilt. How could I be certain?

My more empowered Mom, who claimed her spiritual authority, had taught me to claim my own. It became clearer to me that Mom had handed down to me a deep spiritual connection. Just as that connection guided her life, it guides mine. Mom made decisions for her life that were not fully understood or embraced by others, or sometimes not even herself. This is my truth too. After almost twenty years of running away from my spiritual calling, I had grown into a greater willingness to step into an unknown journey with God. At that point in my life, I had experienced many auditory messages from God. There was a clear pattern to them. Number One, they were messages I did not want to hear, embrace, or act upon. Number Two, despite Number One, I experienced a wave of inner peace.

The message for me to attend seminary in New York met the Number-One criterion I used to discern if a message is from God. I did not want to attend seminary, and I never liked New York. After several months of emotional back-and-forth in my sense of what I was to do, the peace about

Part I: Caring

the unknown for both my life and Mom's continued to grow. Number Two was satisfied. I kept feeling a strong push for me to move to New York, and so I did.

Throughout my first year in seminary, every day my attention was divided between the new studies and activities I was engaging in and my long-distance care and concern for my mother. I traveled frequently to Baltimore to oversee her care. During my semester breaks, I accompanied her on senior excursions she wanted to take since she was no longer able to travel on her own.

In my second year in seminary, I moved Mom to New York to live with me. For a while, having her with me calmed my anxiety since I could see her and care for her each day. She and I were both blessed by the amazing support and love she received from a community of students, staff, and faculty at Union and many of the ministers and members of Riverside Church. Even with that support, it grew increasingly apparent Mom needed more structured care than I could provide. Additionally, not being in her own home was increasingly disorienting for her.

My attention was constantly divided between caring for my mother, working, and studying. I am not certain if I did any of these things well as I was tired and distracted all the time. Mom had said that I was "Momma's company," but I was more her caregiver (doing things for her) than her daughter (being her companion). Additionally, her other three children and all her friends were in Baltimore, and I began recognizing that not seeing them left a longing in her that she could not cognitively understand herself. Seeing them more regularly was stabilizing for her. It was agonizing for me, but I moved her back to Baltimore.

Once again, I pleaded with God to make it clear to me if I were to move to Baltimore with her. And once again, I received a message in my spirit that I was to stay in New York. My heart ached because I believed I was the one who was called to care for the little girl she had become.

For several months, I traveled to Baltimore twice a month. One time, the day before I was to visit her, Mom told me she had a skin rash she wanted me to look at. When I arrived the next day and examined her skin, I discovered not a rash but a patch of dry skin that had formed because she could no longer bathe herself well. On another visit, I looked at Mom's feet and saw severe burns and blisters. She had no recollection of how those burns happened or when. Despite the supports my brothers and I had put in place for Mom, it was clear Mom needed even more to keep her safe. It was time to move Mom into a nursing home.*

Although my brothers agreed with my assessment of her needs, none of them investigated possible placements. Online and in person I researched nursing homes with dementia units. Once I narrowed possible placements down to three locations, I insisted that my brothers visit the residences themselves. I told them I did not want to be in the position of any after-the-move critique from them. After each of them visited one or two places, we agreed upon a new home for Mom.

One thing Mom always asked of me was to commit that I would never place her in a nursing home. Her idea of a nursing home was akin to being placed in an orphanage. Here I was doing the one thing she asked me not to do. Even though I knew this was the best place to keep her safe and for her to receive the kind of care she needed twenty-four hours a day, I was convinced this move was traumatizing and perhaps shaving years off her life. The day we moved her there, she was so angry with me she refused to speak to me. Like a little child, she turned her back on me and stormed away. After I left, I sobbed uncontrollably as I felt I had betrayed her. My heart ached in ways I can never describe.* I was convinced she would never forgive me.

nursing home

Cari speaks of her mother's fear of being placed in a nursing home. For my mom, a nursing home was unthinkable. Mom did not verbalize her wishes, but did everything in her power to signal that she would live at home, or with one of us if need be. —Linda

My heart ached in ways I can never describe

It was the day after we moved my mother into the nursing home. I went downstairs in our house to where my mother used to live to survey the space now devoid of her clothes, diapers, medical equipment—and of her prized possessions. It was empty, yet strangely full. It was full with a sense of having completed a season, a season of care. The room witnessed both the joys and fears of caring for my mother. The juggling of work and life commitments that had more balls dropped than in the air, made me feel like I was always disappointing someone at any given time. Having moved my mother into a nursing home, those daily concerns had been outsourced to the professional care of the staff. I let out a breath that I didn't know I had been holding for years.

At the same time, sadness, longing, and loss also fully occupied the room. I missed seeing her every morning as I prepared her favorite breakfast. I missed tucking her into bed after giving her a bath as she chatted incessantly until her eyes could no longer hold back the sleep. Her scent, her touch, and the various markers of her presence lingered like faint ghost-like presence. I missed the quotidian ritual of duty and love.

On the first evening in her nursing home, my mother would not sleep. She wandered the hallways looking for me, opening every door. My mother demanded that the nurse call me to come and get her. She was certain that there was some mistake. In our subsequent visits, she would get an expectant mischievous glint in her eyes and would say, "Maybe, today, I come with you. Maybe, I can go sleep in your house today." She would try to talk me into bringing her home.

In these moments, I felt that I was abandoning her over and over again. "My heart ached in ways I can never describe." These feelings would chip away at my sense of existential goodness. I was a bad person. I was a bad daughter. I was bad. It became hard for me to even contemplate seeing her because the separation was so hard. My partner, Kathy, would be the one to encourage the visits when I was paralyzed by this all-consuming guilt. My heart was tethered to hers, and hers to mine. With each separation, I left a piece of my heart with her.

Even now, many years later, the guilt of abandoning her returns with such presence. It haunts. It lingers. It hovers. And it tethers me to my mother, lest I forget her. —Su

When I arrived the next morning, Mom, who refused to speak to me the night before, greeted me with a big smile, handwave, and pep in her step. "Hi Babygirl! I like this new apartment you found for me! Thank you!" As I hugged her, I held back my tears so she would not think something was wrong. Tears of relief. Tears of disbelief. Tears of thanksgiving. As Mom had forgotten her anger, pain, and fear from the day before and was gleefully happy in the present moment, I worked to set aside the pain and fear that gripped me the previous night. I joined her in delighting in a brand-new moment in her new home.

Mom lived in the nursing home for seven years, until her death. The care she received there was wonderful. In her early years there, she assisted the staff in leading songs and caring for "the old people," as she called them. She could tell who was sad and comforted them. She felt loved and respected by the staff, and her family and friends were able to visit her regularly. The quality of my visits was enhanced by not having to focus so much attention on the logistics of her care. She and I were simply able to enjoy our time together. We went for walks. We sang together. She showed me her artwork—coloring in the lines. I was her company and she mine.

Even though I could no longer have deep conversations with her about critical issues in my life, Mom continued to teach me and guide me.* One day, while she and I were eating in a restaurant, she was using her hands to get her food as she was beginning to forget how to use eating utensils. Imagining what other restaurant patrons were thinking, at first, I urged her "Mom, you taught me to use my fork, why don't you use yours?" She used it for a few seconds and began using her hands again. Then I shifted my attention to the indignity I imagined about that moment to how much Mom was enjoying her food. It was a sacred moment of learning as Mom invited me to focus on the nurturing and fulfilling possibilities in each moment and not be distracted by worries and imaginings of what others are or might be thinking. Since that lesson from my mother, every time I begin wondering what others might be thinking about me, I remember that holy moment in the restaurant with Mom, and I bring myself back to the things that are most important for my life.

---

teach me and guide me

My mother also continued to teach me.

One summer I travelled out of the country for a couple of weeks. I engaged an elder care social worker to be available for emergencies. When I returned, I learned that one night my mother had diarrhea, fell on the way to the bathroom and was unable to get up. She lay in her own mess until morning. I was devastated by the image of my fragile and fastidious mother lying helpless and soiled on the carpeted floor all night alone.

I visited her as soon as I returned and cried. "Mommy, I'm so sorry I wasn't there for you. To help you when you fell. So sorry." She looked at me with such tenderness and said, "Bobbi, it's all right. I'm an old lady."

Those simple words and her equanimity taught me so much: to accept the inevitable process of aging, to know that hard things are going to happen as the body fails, and to meet even the moments of indignity with grace. —Bobbi

Part I: Caring

Another lesson Mom taught me was about gratitude. When she was losing her memory of how to chew her food, some of her food was pureed. Even then, she would say, "This is the best food I've ever had." Mom taught me to be grateful for the smallest and simplest of things. Living in gratitude has given me a depth of joy that is constant no matter the circumstances of my life.

When my brother called to tell me Mom had stopped eating, knowing how much she enjoyed food, I knew Mom would be dying soon. I hopped on the train to Baltimore early the next morning. When I arrived at the nursing home, she got out of her chair and greeted me, "Hi Babygirl!" Those were the last words she spoke to anyone. She died three days later.

After all my ambivalence through the years about how to be in relationship with Mom and how best to ensure her care, I knew I had done my best from my heart. As she was dying, I spent the night alone with Mom, listening to good church music, singing her favorite hymns, thanking her for her love, and telling her how excited Dad was going to be to greet her. Alone in the bed with her, I had peace as I held her in my arms when she breathed her last breath. I was Momma's company* after all.

Momma's company

I was brought to tears when reading Cari's description of her mom's final night. My mother, too, loved to sing, not hymns, but traditional Spanish songs. Father Dave's presence with all of us at her bedside was the church connection that she needed, but our singing familiar tunes accompanied by my brother's guitar were the connection to her family (to parents, sisters, and cousins) that she needed. The coming together of rituals of music and prayer was the balm she and we needed in those last hours until she took her last breath. —Linda

BABYGIRL

I held you in my arms as you took your last breath,
Babygirl.

In that moment, it didn't matter that time you let my brother
Push me from your lap and didn't make him get off.
None of the hurts mattered
Not then, my Babygirl.

CARING FOR BABYGIRL

No one held you and adored you when you took your first breath,
first steps and first falls.
But then, I was honored to hold you
in my arms, in your last.

You did not leave as you entered.
You left celebrated and loved.
You left having lived a life that mattered.
You left as my Babygirl.

Floods of memories—one Babygirl about another

Stories of you skating free and powerful with the wind
across the viaduct or "viadock" as you said
Skating from your world alone,
imagining another filled with love.

The day I learned you had been the neighborhood champion
when you overtook me playing jacks.
"Babygirl, I have to teach you how to lose with dignity and grace
And inspire you to learn more, to strengthen your skills."

Babygirl, folks tell me I look like you
Tell me I sing like you
Have your chocolate color
Your love for God

I tell me
To love, grow, learn like you,
To be a spiritual warrior like you—
that's my aim, prayer, and goal, Babygirl.

But now,
Now that you are gone,
who will call me Babygirl?

As I travel viadocks of my life
May I be free and powerful
May I hear your voice in the wind of my heart
still calling me Babygirl.

QUESTIONS FOR REFLECTION

1. In what ways did your mother provide opportunities for new learning and growing while she was declining?

Part I: Caring

2. How did you negotiate your feelings when caring for your mother who had not been emotionally supportive of you, or who did not fully embrace your authentic self?

3. How have you wrestled with honoring your father and your mother?

4

No Digas Nada
(Don't Say Anything)

LINDA JARAMILLO

"*Cosa platicada mal hecha y desbaratada.*"[1]

MOM AND I SECRETLY planned for a time when we could live together, just she and I. However, we kept it quiet to avoid potential objections from my three siblings who had similar ideas of Mom living with one of them. Even after moving three thousand miles away, I never gave up the dream of buying a house that we could share somewhere close to the rest of the family, who all live in Oregon.

I felt so far away when Mom fell and broke her hip, resulting in major surgery that took its toll on her ninety-one-year-old body. Her death just three weeks later sent a shock wave through our family thread. Since her passing in March 2009, sorrow, guilt, and regret are ever present in my grieving process.

Four years earlier, I had answered a call to ministry in Cleveland, Ohio. When I talked to Mom about it, she did her best to understand why

---

1. "Talking about what you are planning to do will ruin your plans." This is one of the many Spanish *dichos* or forms of advice that Mom commonly used.

Part I: Caring

I would do such a thing. I now realize that her deepest fear was that these might be her final years; however, I tucked that possibility safely away. "Don't think about it and it won't happen" seemed like a reasonable way to operate. While not rational or even honest, it was my only way of coping with this huge, life-changing decision and far-away move.

It reminds me of some of the ways that Mom would cope. She was very secretive and kept things inside, refusing to share her deepest feelings and painful memories. It was almost as if she was afraid that opening the wounds would bring forth a flood of emotions that she would be unable to contain. Secret keeping became a way of life. I assumed that family secret keeping was Mom's conscious or unconscious way of coping to maintain family privacy* that was based on shame or embarrassment.

coping to maintain family privacy

> Reading this makes me think about the nonverbal language that my mother used to maintain her sense of privacy. On the whole I experienced her as an emotionally expressive person, equally capable of emoting great love and affection, and irritation and anger at our misbehavior. This was in marked contrast to her silence about things that were personally difficult in her life. Her silence in these moments was nonverbally very clear and makes me think about the protection it might have provided for her.
> —Kathy

Sociologist Karen Vallgårda encourages an appreciation of the complexity of secrets:

> Instead of unequivocally condemning secrets, we might recognise that, although some are harmful, others are useful and, perhaps most importantly, a secret can be enabling and suffocating, protective and oppressive all at once.[2]

As Latinos and Latinas, we grew up knowing that our community would be judged by one person's behavior, so the best defense was to keep it private. I have since come to believe that Mom's secrecy was also the result of racial, gender, and religious oppression.* Secrecy is inextricably linked to individual and community safety and security.

---

2. Vallgårda, "Keeping Secrets."

No Digas Nada (Don't Say Anything)

Mom's secrecy was also the result of racial, gender, and religious oppression

My mother, too, felt constrained. For her, it was by the implicit and explicit rules of her class and religious upbringing. She came from a long lineage of enduring women, women who tolerated a life that did not allow a consideration of their wants on so many levels, a life seemingly preordained for marriage and early motherhood.

How does the age at which a mother dies affect how a daughter responds to a mother's life and her own? Our understanding about another unfolds over time and depends both on what one says as well as on what one does. Unlike Linda's mom, who took such comfort in her children and family, I imagine my mother struggled, being a young mother, with the ongoing burden of raising three children with limited financial resources and not a lot to look forward to. I will always wonder what secrets my mom held about her life that could not be spoken lest they be felt, or even more dangerously, acted upon.

It is a wonder to read Linda's and other sisters' experiences in witnessing their mothers transform from young parents to grandmothers/elders; to witness the changes in how their mothers showed up for the later years of their lives; to read about how they cared for their daughters as young women and, in the end of their lives, were lovingly attended to by their devoted daughters. The arc of my mom's life was short. Not being able to witness the possibilities for transformation for her and for our relationship is at the heart of my grief. Yet even as I write this, I imagine my arms outstretched, fingertips touching the place where her life ends and offering all I have done and all I will become as an extension of the semicircle of who she was/is. —Laura

As we were growing up, I remember times when Mom's spirit seemed to lose its luster. Her intelligence was suppressed. Her self-confidence depleted. However, she came back to life when she courageously launched her career in education and rented her own apartment when others would normally be retiring. She went on to live independently until her death at the age of ninety-one. During her final thirty years, when she was confident that the environment was safe, the stories Mom had safely tucked away began to pour out of her.

During my early childhood years, we lived on a farm in southern Colorado where my father was the hired hand. Mom's role as housewife limited her interactions with friends and neighbors, and connections to other families were infrequent. Thankfully, there were periodic times of joy when family gathered, especially when Mom's two sisters were around. They whispered stories (maybe secrets) and privately giggled. All three had beautiful voices, so when our large extended family gathered, singing the traditional songs of our heritage filled the air with pride and liberating spirit that held us tightly within the family circle.

My parents were in their midforties and I was entering high school when we moved off the farm and into town at the other end of the San Luis Valley. While the move was only forty miles from the farm, it seemed like much farther from the segregated community where we had been. It was closer to New Mexico, where the culture of our ancestry was much more apparent and appreciated. We heard Spanish spoken in the stores, in our neighborhood, and even in church. At school, we had teachers who looked like us, and we were finally recognized as leaders.

Mom's sisters were our new next-door neighbors! Mom went to work outside the home and began to feel a sense of pride in contributing to the family income. While most of my parents' friends were family, Mom made some of her own friends outside that constricted circle. There is no doubt that her self-confidence was being realized in new ways.

One by one, our family unit migrated northwest to Oregon nearly a decade later. We discovered that Oregon was populated by a vast majority of white folks. Thankfully, we had regained our authentic consciousness of cultural traditions and values, so we were able to resist assimilation.

Unfortunately, among those traditions, the roles of husband and wife were deeply engrained. My parents' Roman Catholic and Latino upbringing reinforced the expectation that the man was the head of the household, denying any possibility of a marriage based on the value and power of each member of the partnership. With that backdrop, my father exercised his role in domineering, demanding, and controlling ways. Mom was trapped by her inability to challenge the circumstances, and leaving was not an option due to family and community expectations complicated by economic circumstances.

Mom and Dad finally separated under difficult circumstances, but because they were Catholic, they never divorced. Mom remained resentful, angry, and bitter for many years. However, as time passed, their relationship seemed to evolve into a mutually respectful one. Months later, Dad moved into his own place in the same apartment complex where Mom lived, and they learned to be much more harmoniously connected while apart. She

No Digas Nada (Don't Say Anything)

was finally free to think for herself and determine her own life course. She began to talk about that life.

As noted, Mom lived independently for nearly thirty years in her sixties, seventies, eighties, and into her ninety-first year. As a Roman Catholic, Mom was committed to the rituals of the Church. She may have missed the Latin Mass but really appreciated it when English and Spanish made it much more accessible. Her prayer life was very private. Reciting the Rosary was an expected practice when families were experiencing grief from the loss of a loved one. Novenas, which are prayed for nine days to patron saints for particular needs (in sickness, for healing, during and after tragedy or loss, for hope or in gratitude or joy), were commonplace for Mom.[3] Her legendary style of keeping things to herself and demanding personal privacy surfaced from time to time. She lived alone and took care of herself by employing her religious practices and using natural ancestral remedies. She refused to go to the doctor for general care.

It wasn't until she suffered a slight stroke in her eighties, landing her in the emergency room, that she was forced to get medical attention. During her hospitalization for the stroke, her examination exposed serious heart problems. Mom was blessed to have a Latino cardiologist who was not only tremendously competent in his specialization but also knew from his own cultural heritage and upbringing how Mom's perspectives should be revered and respected. Her need for personal privacy was being challenged by the necessity to share beyond her comfort level. There was no need to explain any of that to Dr. Reyes. He simply got it. He knew that Mom was the matriarch of our family (on her side) and recognized her role as the wisdom leader who embodied the significance of our legacy. It was a relief to know that we did not have to provide cultural lessons as her health history was being revealed. The gift of cultural and language competence from medical caregivers should never go unrecognized or unappreciated. It is further proof that cultural practices are critical to a holistic understanding of our emotional, spiritual, and physical well-being.

When Dr. Reyes's examinations showed that Mom was going to need a complex heart surgery, he went about finding a nationally recognized surgeon to perform it. Dr. Reyes assured Mom that he would accompany her and find someone who would fully understand her anxieties and cultural values. Thankfully that surgeon practiced at a hospital near her home. As Dr. Reyes and the surgeon together explained the procedure to our sibling

---

3. For full list of novenas, see https://catholicnovenaapp.com/list-of-all-novenas/#.

Part I: Caring

foursome, they assured us that our perspectives would be heard while reminding us that the last word would be Mom's.

The formerly meek, passive, and obedient Louise Jaramillo had grown her wings. Mom verbalized her fear, named her hesitation, took control, and exercised her decision-making authority. It appeared that her former practice of keeping secrets was lessening; it was refreshing to watch. She wanted to hear our opinions, but she courageously took charge and asked her own questions.

She asked the surgeon why he would perform such a complicated surgery on someone her age. His immediate response was, "Why not?" He added that he had done a similar surgery on his eighty-six-year-old mother the year before. Without missing a beat, Mom questioned the ethics of operating on your own mother. He understood her concern, saying that given the choice, there was no way he was going to let anyone else touch his mom. He promised to care for our mother the way he cared for his.

She came through the surgery with flying colors! Recovery was a different story.

Mom expected to bounce back and resume her independent lifestyle in short order. Her hospital stay was much longer than planned because she was weak and discouraged, with little energy to do the walking and physical therapy prescribed. As we journeyed with her, my older sisters and I had different approaches to supporting Mom. They insisted that she should do what she was told if she expected to regain her physical strength. I believed that this insistence only made her more discouraged about her slow recovery, so I defended her.

I am the youngest sibling and was the last to leave home,* with Dad working outside the area, so Mom and I lived alone together for over a year during my passage into adulthood. It was a special time of getting to know each other at a much deeper level which had a significant impact on my formation. Mom was now facing life-altering circumstances of her own at a later phase of life. At the same time, I was preparing for ministry and immersed in pastoral care training, so I relied on learned practices grounded in listening, empathy, and spiritual care. It was apparent that my sisters and I were not in agreement on which methods would produce the results that were needed for Mom's recovery. Our differences of opinion increased pressure on our mother.* I quickly recognized how subjective it is to exercise objective pastoral care practices with a family member. I was reminded that the best approach would be to take a step back and reclaim my role as her youngest child.

No Digas Nada (Don't Say Anything)

I am the youngest sibling and was the last to leave home

Like Linda, I am the youngest of four children. And for a few years before leaving home for college, I too enjoyed spending time with my mom and dad without having to negotiate with my siblings for one-on-one time with our parents. Having those few years with their daily attention just for me was extraordinary. Well, at least when I wanted it.

It is often said that God calls the young because they are strong and the old because they are wise. I saw my parents grow in wisdom as they got older. In the earlier years of their parenting, Mom and Dad were often judgmental of my brothers and me. By the time I was the only child still living at home, they both had begun to mellow and were more able to trust that their teaching would help me to make choices that were right for me. As Mom and Dad grew more mature, they had a greater capacity to let their children make our choices without their judgment or intervention. As the youngest child, I benefitted more from their emotional and spiritual growth. The major factor in my parents' maturing was Mom's personal empowerment. —Cari

Our differences of opinion increased pressure on our mother

It is so different to care for an aging parent as an only child. As I read Linda's chapter, I was moved alternately by the warm and nourishing experience of living within a large, vibrant, involved family and by the difficulties of having significant disagreements with siblings about the how to care for their mother. Though I longed to have siblings for most of my life, when caring for my mother, I was glad for the freedom to do what I thought best, without having to seek approval, convince, negotiate or argue with anyone.

I've heard so many stories about the conflicts between siblings when making complex decisions about a parent's care. While there are opportunities for healing and a celebration of life as families gather around an aging and dying elder, rivalries and other difficult dynamics can be resurrected when the family system is stressed by caregiving.

Torah stories portray both the possibility for healing and the cementing of rivalries when a parent is aged or dying. Isaac and Ishmael come together to bury Abraham, signaling that they had reached some reconciliation. The rivalry between Jacob and Esau is further entrenched when Isaac gives the blessing meant for Esau to the younger Jacob. The rivalries between Joseph and his brothers are resolved at the end of Jacob's life, but only because one sibling, Joseph, has risen to such a position of power that he can orchestrate the ending of family conflict as he chooses. —Bobbi

Mom was finally discharged, and we launched the family plan for caregiving in her home. We were blessed with assistance from a dear friend and beloved health care worker (Judy) during the day. As we rotated care, Mom's evenings were complicated by each of our definitive styles. Even having been reared in the same household, learning the same values, we had distinct approaches and a wide range of opinions about care and connection.*

care and connection

We practice care not because we are connected; rather, we become connected because we practice care. In Korean culture, the Confucian virtue of filial piety is central to how we live and organize ourselves as a society. Filial piety is an unconditional obligation to respect and care for our parents and our ancestors. It is the right order of the cosmos that maintains harmony. We respect and care for parents, not because we love them, or because they are deserving, but because it is the right thing to do.

As a feminist, I have resisted this virtue because it centered on male lineage that privileged father–son relationships. And while the responsibility of duty fell on a son, it was the wife or the daughters who did the work of caring.

But caring for my mother with Alzheimer's over an extended period of time shifted my perspective. Caring creates unforeseen connections. When I observe the wave of grief that gripped me after my mother's passing, it is my mother with Alzheimer's whom I miss the most: her delight in a mouthful of ice cream, the dream stories she told, her one trouser leg that was always up while the other one was down, and her favorite pair of colorful socks. These memories are what send pangs of loss to my heart. In caring for her, I was growing with her. During the intense years of caring for my mother, I came to know my mother in intimate and vulnerable ways. It is a rare privilege to know one's mother in this way.

In my office, I have a Korean calligraphy artwork that looks like two people kneeling and holding hands viewed from the side angle. It is an artistic rendering of the Korean word, "효" (*hyo*), which means filial piety. And inside the letter is the inscription from Exod 20:12, the fifth of the Ten Commandments: "Honor

No Digas Nada (Don't Say Anything)

your father and your mother, so that your days may be long in the land that the LORD your God is giving you." (NRSV) It is a daily reminder that I am my mother's daughter not only because she bore me and raised me. I am her daughter because of the bond of care and connection. —Su

Mom and Judy had a special bond and with that came the assurance that their conversations were honest and more objective. It provided a safe and sacred space for Mom to disclose her feelings. Mom's recovery at home went on for many weeks. Some can be attributed to her emotional health condition, but I believe some of it was related to her loneliness. She wanted to remain independent and self-reliant, but she also loved having the company around the clock, even with its inconsistencies.

Mom eventually recovered and went back to her rich and independent life for several more years. We were all relieved that things were getting back to normal. However, her heart condition made me realize that my mom was not going to live forever. I could not imagine how the planet could go on, or how I would survive without her. I wanted her to live as long as I live. I knew it was a selfish notion, but I held it nonetheless. I managed to tuck this underlying fear into the depths of my psyche and did my best to avoid thinking about it. I had learned the skill of secret keeping well.

When I moved three thousand miles away, Mom and I honored our commitment to keep in touch by telephone at least once or twice a week, sometimes more frequently. She stubbornly refused to add voice mail or an answering machine to her phone, so she did not always know how often I tried to call. When I complained that she should get voice mail so I could leave a message, she simply said, "just keep calling," and so I did.

I kept my promise to come home three to four times a year and made a point of staying at her house for a portion of the time, splitting my time with kids and grandkids. I loved every moment of it. Those times are warmly etched in my memory. When we were alone, I would crawl into bed with her,* and we talked about many things. I asked lots of questions. My heart sang because Mom was more open to sharing her story than I had ever heard.

I would crawl into bed with her

I imagine I did as a child, but I have no memories of lying in the bed with my mom until I was fifty years old. Prior to moving to

Part I: Caring

> New York, I had not lived in the same city with Mom since I left for college at age seventeen. When I moved to New York and she was living in a one-bedroom apartment, I had the option of sleeping in the bed with her or on her love seat. For many years, I chose to curl up uncomfortably on the love seat because the idea of sleeping in the bed with my mom felt too intimate to me. As her dementia progressed, and I bathed Mom to wash the parts of her body she no longer knew how to wash clean, all concerns about too much intimacy dissipated. Those concerns were washed away by love. Then the idea of intimacy, sleeping in the same bed with Mom, became very welcome. The experiences of lying in the bed with her became treasured moments. —Cari

She shared how her mother, a teacher, always encouraged her to go to college and told her not to let anything or anyone get in her way. Sadly, my grandmother became ill and died when Mom was only seventeen years old. Because she had two younger sisters, Mom had to assume responsibility for their care at a very young age, so her life course changed, and her dream of going to college was lost.

It was forty years before my mom realized her dream of teaching. She was hired to teach English to Spanish-speaking children and youth. She flourished in her career and is still remembered fondly by many students who have gone on to educational leadership as teachers, principals, and even school superintendents. Other students went on to other professions and still remember what a difference Mom made in their lives. She served in public schools for over twenty years and did not retire until she was eighty-three years old.

She went on to fully enjoy retirement for nearly a decade even when challenges to her physical health presented themselves, with the stroke and heart surgery. She liked to go places and see new things as long as travel did not include an airplane.

On that fateful March day, her granddaughter Luisa and children stopped by for one of their regular visits. Mom was always so cautious, but on this day, as she greeted the kids at the door, she made a quick turn and caught her foot on the carpet landing squarely on her hip. Thank God that Luisa was right there and could call for help. I shudder to think about what would have happened had Mom been alone when she fell.

Doctors advised the family that Mom was going to require surgery to repair her broken hip; otherwise she would need to use a wheelchair indefinitely. For her, immobility was not an option. However, because of her medication due to a previous heart condition, the surgical preparation would require a disruption to her system. She sailed through the procedure successfully and was well on the road to recovery despite the major change in her medication regimen.

I made it home in time for the surgery. We explored continuing rehabilitative care in a nursing facility, which we promised would be only temporary, but I do not think she believed us. I imagine that at the back of her mind was the fear that her independent lifestyle was coming to an end.

Several days later, I was back in Cleveland and struggling to sleep. In my prayer time, it suddenly came upon me that my mom might not make it. The flutter in my heart was palpable; I once again refused to allow that possibility to enter my thinking, afraid that it might be true. Four days later, my brother called me to say that Mom was not doing well, and I should come back as soon as possible. I was on an airplane back to Portland the next day.

When I walked into Mom's hospital room, she was surprised and asked why I had come back so soon. I reminded her of my promise to come back as soon as I could, but I suspect that she knew that things were very serious. Not only was she at risk of losing her independence, but her life might be coming close to an end. In a short time, she was no longer able to make decisions on her own. She retreated to her old ways of not discussing things, holding her thoughts close to her heart, and hiding her fears. Her perpetual survivor instincts resurfaced, accompanied by her secret ways of coping.

Mom's health condition deteriorated because of her inability to eat. Dr. Reyes discovered that Mom had a huge hiatal hernia that was pressing on her digestive system, making it difficult if not impossible to eat much solid food. We questioned why this hiatal hernia had gone undiagnosed, even in open heart surgery. He grieved with us and couldn't give us a good explanation, saying only that there was no way she could endure even a simple surgery to repair it. She was suffering from malnutrition, so Dr. Reyes recommended that we have a feeding tube inserted. After much family deliberation, we finally relented.

Throughout that week, several attending physicians advised us that Mom's kidneys were failing due to the years of medication. Even if she would gain her strength back with the intravenous feeding, her essential organs had begun to give out. We gathered regularly in her hospital room throughout the day and night. She was never alone. It was not unusual for her biological and spiritual children, grandchildren, great-grandchildren, nieces, and nephews to hold vigil inside and outside her room.

On one occasion, a nurse noted that we had too many people in the room, only to be reminded by my eldest sister that it was our intent to stay. She promised that we would do our best to not interrupt needed medical care; however, we would stay. We worked out ways to respect each other's needs—our need for family connection and their need to provide the best possible medical care. It was an important cultural values lesson for this nurse and the rest of the medical staff.

The week went by and doctors continued to advise that we should consult with one another and consider hospice care.* Only Dr. Reyes disagreed, saying that she had weathered serious health challenges in the past. He yearned for her to survive just as much as we did. It must have been in closed physicians' consultations that he became convinced and ultimately advised us that her quality of life would undoubtedly be seriously jeopardized.

> **hospice care**
>
> A few years ago, I was a founding partner in the creation of What Matters: Caring Conversations about End of Life. The program is part of Respecting Choices, which guides people in advance-care planning. While I understand that many people do not feel comfortable having conversations about their wishes, I have witnessed the comfort that having those conversations brings, knowing that the people who love you will be guided by your own values and wishes if you ever can't make a decision for yourself. Linda's mom's story is inspiring, as the family walked with her with each new development. Because of a culture of not sharing, the family needed to examine what they knew—both from what was spoken and done, and from what was not revealed. —Mychal

The hospice care team helped us understand that Mom was enduring unnecessary medical trauma. As the days passed, she became nonresponsive. We made the choice to take her home and journey with her for the last days. Our vigil continued around the clock over the weekend. Our family was together—from the youngest to the eldest. Children running through the house stopped by Mom's bed to kiss her hands. The smells of familiar food filtered through the house.

No Digas Nada (Don't Say Anything)

Father Dave, Mom's parish priest came as we surrounded her bed, telling stories and singing her favorite songs. We laughed at how our recollections of childhood did not match up. I suspect that Mom was just shaking her head as she listened, even though we couldn't see her doing so. Just three weeks after her accident, my beloved mother passed away on Sunday morning, March 22, 2009, at the age of ninety-one, surrounded by her children and a few grandchildren. There was nothing more holy than ushering the one who gave me life out of her life on earth, on to life universal.

Mom was a lifelong, devout Catholic, so there was no question that we would follow the Catholic Church's traditional practices of a Rosary recitation and a full Catholic funeral Mass and burial, with each sibling participating in our own way. When Father Dave came to discuss the plans, his generous spirit and gentle nature was a great comfort to each of us. He remembered that I am an ordained Christian minister and asked me to participate in the communion ritual and to serve with him. I was stunned. After I had been denied the Catholic Eucharist for decades, it was heartwarming to receive such a generous invitation. Father reassured us that he was convinced that Mom would not have it any other way.

Extended family and friends filled the St. Anthony's sanctuary along with many of her neighbors, former students, and school colleagues. Mom was a respected, honored, and revered wise elder far beyond her family circle. She was Tía (Auntie) and Abuelita (Grandma) far beyond biological parameters. Mom was the glue that held us together.

She was our *encuentro*. *Encuentro* is the Spanish word for "encounter"; however, in Spanish it has a much deeper meaning. *Encuentro* is the experience of having little or no space between us as beings. It is the understanding that when we meet in an *encuentro*, it is difficult if not impossible to know where one person ends and the other begins. While we are separate and distinct human beings, we have a genuine connection that is impossible to describe. The ancestral stories that Mom told us provide a bridge to the *encuentro* between past, present, and future generations.

Every family member of Mom's generation has now passed on.

In the summer of 2019, we (siblings, cousins, children, and grandchildren) gathered near our childhood homes in the San Luis Valley of Colorado. We shared old stories, sang the usual songs, cooked the food that has nourished our bodies through the years. We laughed and cried together as we grieved the loss of our parents and of some siblings from our generation.

Part I: Caring

We learned how each of our sibling groups had come together in their own ways to provide compassionate care to our beloved parents, all of which included the rituals and cultural practices of generations past. We remembered how Mom and her sisters used to whisper secrets to each other and giggle. We also recalled that our parents instilled a sense of pride in our history, albeit it coupled with the importance of humility and privacy. We are deeply grateful for all that they taught us but confessed that we do not feel smart enough or wise enough to carry the torch for the generations that follow us.

I now live back home in Portland.

My memories of Mom remain vivid. I remember how smart my Mom was about so many things. I remember her doing the *New York Times* crossword puzzle until just two weeks before she died. I remember all the things we talked about and the times I called to ask for advice. I remember that even though I was sixty years old, I could crawl into bed with her and we would watch her favorite TV shows. I remember our plans to live together. My mom continues to be a significant role model as I journey through life. I miss her daily but thank God that every now and then she appears in my dreams with some sort of lesson that I need to learn.

Louise Consuelo Marquez Jaramillo, fondly known as Luisa, was proud of the fact that she lived on her own at the age of ninety-one. While lonely at times, she enjoyed her home, her neighborhood, her family, her friends, and her work colleagues, many of whom visited her regularly. She was consistently surrounded by people who loved and respected her. Her brilliant mind and capacity to remember so many family stories was a gift. Mom engaged in conversations and certainly shared her opinions, but through the years I am continually reminded that her secrecy was inextricably linked to her own safety and security.

¡LUISA JARAMILLO—PRESENTE!

QUESTIONS FOR REFLECTION

1. Do you remember being told not to share certain information about your family (to keep a secret)? Looking back on it, how would you describe that experience?

No Digas Nada (Don't Say Anything)

2. How would you describe your childhood growing up with siblings (immediate family, cousins, close relatives)? How are your stories similar and how are they different from the ones others tell?

3. Were the health care providers that were involved in your parent's care from the same race or ethnic background as your parent? Were caregivers able to converse in your parent's preferred language? How did that impact their interactions and relationship?

INTERLUDE

Picturing Our Mothers

(From left) Mary Breitman holding Bobbi; Grandmother Chana/Anna Radoff; Aunt Rose Thaler with my cousin Joan, holding the doll. In front of a Bronx apartment building circa 1952.

Bess Merola Talvacchia with Kathy in Fairmount Park, Philadelphia, circa 1959.

Gladys Jackson holding Cari after attending church. Baltimore 1957.

Linda with Louise Jaramillo. Pacific School of Religion commencement, Berkeley, California. May 2005.

Marilyn D'Elia O'Loughlin holding Laura, Janet, and Debbie.
Hempstead, New York. March 1963.

Kim Yang Sook holding Su. Seoul, South Korea, circa 1962.

Tova Springer circa 1967 holding daughters Tamar (left) and Mychal.

PART II

Grieving

5

A Voice Calling Back

LAURA O'LOUGHLIN

WHEN DEATH ARRIVES AT our home, it can feel as if we are whisked away from life as we know it and plunged into an altered state of reality. In this place, we navigate the intense physical and psychic process of grieving. This grief can take many forms—tears, numbness, anger, disorientation, even temporary madness. If we are graced, we may find the possibility of a heightened sense of aliveness, gratitude, connection, and love. Difficult as it may be, the act of working with the energy of grieving is essential to finding a way back to our new home, one without the physical presence of our loved one.

Ritual is a medicine for these moments. It offers us a way to traverse this sacred journey of death by creating a space for us to be held in the intensity of devastating loss. Rituals are intentional symbolic activities designed to offer a path of healing and connection to something deeper and wider than our heartache. Rituals are not just found in traditional communal offerings but can also be private, spontaneous enactments.

When my mother died, I had no cultural, religious, or family rituals to guide me, no connection to community, nor family members who knew how to offer solace to a young woman who had just lost a parent. In turn, the pain of losing my mother became a frozen grief, quietly haunting me for over four decades.

Part II: Grieving

It is, however, never too late to care for our grief. With the support of Zen Buddhist practice and this "sisters in mourning" group, I began to listen, acknowledge, and feel into this locked-away sorrow. And it was from this listening that I found the ritual of writing to my mother. It helped me honor my pain, make sense of my loss, and bring me back to her. For those of you who feel your grief is too much to bear, I hope my ritual* will offer you encouragement in finding your own.

---

my ritual

When my mother died, we had the traditional formal ritual of a wake, funeral service, and burial at the gravesite. Seeing my mother's coffin being lowered in the ground was an important marker of transition from an ambiguous loss that had accompanied me for years as she was slipping deeper into Alzheimer's to a sense of finality, of having completed a journey. And everyday rituals had been my medicine for each of the losses that presented themselves to me.

During those years of caring for my mother, the everyday rituals were both of *doing* and *not doing*. My daily ritual of getting up early to prepare breakfast for my parents before going to work was a ritual of *doing*. The daily ritual of untangling my mother's yarn after work was another ritual of *doing*. My mother was an expert knitter, but she no longer remembered her lifelong passion. Instead, she would tangle up the yarn in her attempt to knit. After my day's work, I untangled the yarn one strand at a time, without snipping loose the tightly wound knots.

The everyday rituals of *not doing* were the rituals we stop doing, or what we did instead because the *doing* was not possible. My mother's beautiful model hands were always manicured in red polish. Every other week I took my mother to the nail salon to get her nails done. She remembered to hold her hands still until the polish dried even though she could not remember how to eat. But there came a time when she could not keep her wet polish from smudging, unable to sit still while the polish dried. So, we moved from the regular polish to gel polish. A ritual of *not doing*. She enjoyed this for a while until she began to ingest chipped gel nail polish. So, we stopped painting her nails altogether. Another ritual of *not doing*. Instead, I began to massage her hands with cream. These rituals of *not doing* were, in retrospect, rituals of letting go and letting in. With each loss of function or memory, there were corresponding rituals of letting go. But the loss was not just a loss. It was an invitation for letting in a new Mom who was becoming. —Su

A Voice Calling Back

Weds. Jan. 30, (1980)
Dear Laura,

Got your letter today and was very glad to hear from you. The other night I dreamt you were a little girl again (about 8 or 9 years old). It wasn't the first time. Actually, it was the fourth time in the last couple of months. I wonder what it means. Probably just wishful dreaming. If you don't come down, it will be a total of three months before we see you. Be good and keep writing your mother...

Love, Mom

March, 2020
Dear Mom,

I am trying to reach across almost forty years of separation and find you again. To figure out who you were and who I was with you. It saddens me that all I have left of you are some fuzzy memories and a handful of letters. Letters from when you were a teenager and then again when I was a teenager and we wrote each other after I first left for college. Although all memories of you evoke sadness in me, I hold tightly onto these fragments to keep you from disappearing completely.

I have no deeply felt sense of you in my body. Living so many decades without you and seeing you last through a teen's eyes, my memories of you are as murky and faded as the few remaining photos I have of us.

This is part of the legacy of a mother leaving her daughter too soon. I was too young to ask all the questions I now desperately want to know, and I was too young for you to share the enormity of what you were going through.* When you died, you took your stories with you forever. Dad's

Part II: Grieving

body tensed up in pain at the mention of your name; I learned not to speak to him about you at all. Whenever I could muster the courage to ask your mom or your sister about you, I could feel it trigger a grief that rendered them mute for a moment, after which they spoke of you in vague generalities, shrinking the complexity of your being into an anemic, easily digestible version they could bear to share.

I was too young for you to share the enormity of what you were going through

It has been deeply moving to witness Laura's journey of listening, acknowledging, and feeling into her "locked-away sorrow." Through our writing, all the sisters in mourning had the experience of reaching deeper levels of understanding of ourselves, our mothers, and our mother–daughter relationships. But Laura had to take the deepest dive into the unknown, to find words for what had been wordless.

Reading Laura's chapter plunged me into deep reflection about the experience of my daughters, whom I adopted after their mother died, not only too soon, but in a sudden and violent way. My younger daughter was seven years old, going into first grade, when she came to live with me. She was still a little girl and was longing for a mommy. That was not so for her teenage sister.

As I struggled with the shock of my then husband's sudden death and the responsibilities of becoming a single parent a year after the girls came to live with me, I know I was unable to encompass the enormity of the many losses and traumas that my thirteen-to-fourteen-year-old daughter was going through. Not only did she lose her mother in a shocking way, but being placed with me in Philadelphia was not her choice. She had to leave the foster family to whom she had become attached and move across country to a place utterly unfamiliar to her. Though I loved my daughters deeply from the start and never broke faith with them, I regret the times I was reactive to my older daughter's understandable ambivalence toward me.

Laura's chapter gave me such a valuable glimpse into the inchoate turmoil at the heart of a teenage girl living through her mother's suffering and incomprehensible death at just the time she is trying to figure out who she is, how to live her own life and make her own choices. Reading Laura's chapter leaves me with many unanswered questions about how my daughters' lives have been shaped by their mother's early death, beyond what I might understand or perhaps what they can express to me. —Bobbi

Here is what I do know. You were the daughter of poor Italian immigrants who came to this country as children near the turn of the century. You spent your childhood in Greenpoint, Brooklyn, surrounded by extended family who gathered at Grandpa's candy store to talk and play cards. Grandma made you special egg creams with extra eggs in it because she thought you were too skinny. You were smart and beautiful and had lots of boyfriends, sometimes more than one at the same time. You became a wife and mother at seventeen, a teenager yourself. You hid your pregnancy from your father, had a shotgun wedding, and moved to Florida for your first year of marriage to blur the date of your first child's birth. By the age of twenty-two you had three young daughters while working full-time as a clerk. You lived in the suburbs of Long Island with a husband who carpooled into the city each evening to do his overnight shift as a New York City subway cop.

Then, at the age of thirty-eight, you were plunged into the world of cancer,* which in 1979 meant crude, experimental treatments and harsh side effects that were mostly left untreated. These are the most vivid memories I have of you.

---

at the age of thirty-eight, you were plunged into the world of cancer

Laura shared that her mother became a mother when she was seventeen years old and died just two decades later at the young age of thirty-eight, when Laura herself was only eighteen. For most of us, losing our mother is a shattering experience, but losing her at such a young age intensifies the trauma at a critical time of fragile emotional maturity.

As I reflected on Laura's memories, I was reminded that my grandmother died at the age of thirty-seven, leaving my mom motherless when she was only seventeen. It took many years for my mom to talk much about her mother; as I hear Laura's story, I realize that Mom's memories were too painful, and the grief was too great to allow them to surface.

All I remember hearing is that Grandma had a very weak heart and she died of congestive heart failure. Grandma's sisters insisted that she live with them rather than with her own husband and children. Their reasoning was that taking care of her children was too taxing on her heart. I cannot imagine how Mom and her sisters must have felt at hearing that they might be the cause of Grandma's failing health. She died before ever coming back home to live with them.

Part II: Grieving

> I never knew my grandmother but admired her through a
> beautiful picture that always hung in our home. —Linda

The cancer cast such a dark, scary pall over our home. We all suffered alone and in silence within the same house—you weak and in pain in the bedroom; Dad lying on the couch in the living room with one hand cupped over his face trying to nap before work; me lying quietly on my bed, feeling distressed and frozen at the same time; my sisters, Janet and Debbie, nearby but in their uneasiness far away.

I remember one day you were lying in bed ill and clearly in tremendous pain, and without turning to look at me you said, "I don't worry about you; I know you will be okay." One simple sentence. Yet I have held onto these words like they were a rare find in an architectural dig, using them to piece together something about myself and the nature of our relationship, who I was to you and even how those few words may have shaped who I came to be. That sentence has alternatively comforted and haunted me. Letting me know that there is something sturdy and resilient inside of me has been reassuring, and I imagine might have been reassuring for you too at the moment. Heartbreaking for a teen with a childlike need to have her mother demonstrate the depth of her love by the depth of her worry.

I remember you telling me how you wanted to live long enough to see me graduate from college, the first one in our family to do so. We were all heartbroken that day, and although we tried to celebrate, all I could feel wearing my cap and gown was a sad gaping hole created by your absence.

Although I am now fifty-eight, having lived close to two decades longer than you had a chance to, the feelings that arise in me when I attempt to speak to you are those of a bereft child, with emotions as raw as if you had died yesterday. As grief is wont to do, these painful feelings come unbidden, erupting when witnessing a touching scene between a mother and daughter, or when recognizing there is no mother to turn to as I navigate intimate rites of passage as a woman, like menopause. Sometimes they come with no apparent precipitant at all. I hadn't a clue to the depth of this fault line within me until I joined my sisters in mourning and began to explore what it was like to lose you. I am only now just beginning to uncover how your illness and death shaped my life in ways beyond what I could ever truly understand or articulate.

A Voice Calling Back

Because I never got a chance to tell you these things, it feels good to write you now* as if you were sitting across from me or alive still in some other town opening a letter from your grown daughter in between visits.

Love you,
Laura

---

it feels good to write to you now

Laura's letters to her mother have made me think about the practice that I was engaging in writing my own chapter, that is, the practice of mentoring. I wrote to my young self in a way that was meant to provide the wisdom and experience that a mentor can provide when a young person is encountering difficult life experiences. I sought to mentor my young self in a way that I wish I had been mentored by someone at that time. —Kathy

~

Sat. Feb. 21, (1981)
Dear Laura,

As you could tell by my voice on the phone, you know I was very upset with you. In four weeks, all we got was one letter from you. Then on Sunday, I call, you're not there. The least you could have done was to send me a note instead of having me waste a call from Florida. The next night when your roommate told me to call, the line was busy. Then you call at an expensive time of the night and expect me to call you back. It just goes to show how often you think of us.

Your mother

March 2020
Dear Mom,

As I write this,* the country is in a virtual lockdown in an attempt to limit the destruction of a worldwide pandemic. In 1918, when your mom was just eight years old, her mom died from a pandemic flu. Seems Grandma and I share this legacy of motherless daughter.

As I write this

> In the midst of the COVID-19 pandemic, the world of 1918 feels so close. We can no longer assume even the small measure of control that felt attainable in our choices about caring and grieving back in 2019. Having worked in the hospital throughout the height of the pandemic in New York in the spring and summer of 2020, I have a new appreciation for what it means to live with the widespread fear of contagion and of death coming quickly on an unfathomably large scale. One text that has accompanied me is from Mishnah Sanhedrin 4:5. This text explores why it is that all human beings are descendants of a single human being—Adam. We learn from this that each person contains a whole world. When one of us dies, a whole world dies. And the text continues: "humans stamp many coins with one seal and they are all like one another; but the King of kings, the Holy Blessed One, has stamped every human with the seal of the first human being, yet not one of them are like another. Therefore, everyone must say, 'For my sake was the world created.'"[1] Every day, as I walked by the refrigerated trailers that contained the bodies of people who had died, too many bodies to fit in the morgue, too many people to be picked up by funeral homes and buried or cremated, I thought to myself, "When one of us dies, a whole world dies." I prayed for the worlds contained in the trailers, praying for them to find peace even in the protracted transition from this world to the next, accompanied by so many others who had died alongside them. And I prayed for the families who could not be with them in the hospital to care for them at the end of their lives, and for the families who could not grieve for them in community because of social distancing. So many of the rituals and obligations which we have described lovingly in this book have been unavailable to those who have been affected by COVID-19, highlighting what a gift it is to be able to care for and mourn for the people we love. —Mychal

As I think about you and me, my mind keeps turning toward an indigenous understanding of trauma. That the histories of our peoples live in our bodies, in our nervous systems. How did her losing her mother so young live in Grandma, and how did her lack of "mother knowing" affect how

---

1. Mishnah Sanhedrin 4:5

she raised you and your sister?* How did the poverty and violence of their southern homelands affect their bodies, yours, and now mine?

how did her lack of "mother knowing" affect how she raised you and your sister?

Laura's questions about the impacts of early "motherloss" in her family relate directly to my life. My mother, Gladys, experienced motherloss twice—once at age six when her mother placed her in an orphanage, and again at age fourteen when her mother died. As Laura wondered about the impact of motherloss on how her Grandma parented her mother, I also wonder about the impact of my mother's loss on how she parented my brothers and me. She did not begin her parenting experience with "mother knowing"; rather, there was a lot of on-the-job training. Additionally, Mom learned about mothering through Dad's perspectives about how his mother had parented. I do see differences in my brothers and me, some of which I believe were influenced by changes in Mom's "mother knowing" over the years. The biggest change was learning how to mother each child in ways that supported their individual uniqueness and needs. —Cari

I remember once you looked me in the eyes and declared, "Forget about marrying a doctor or lawyer, become one."* Offering advice about life was such an unusual way for you to speak to me, so those words really stuck. Was this a wish for me to live in a way that was out of reach for you as a first-generation working-class mother in the late 1950s? Was it a centuries-old distrust of depending on men? Was it the weariness in your bones turned into a fantasy of being able to relax and be taken care of by your children? Was it an attempt to ensure I had a direction after you were gone? I will never know exactly what you were trying to tell me nor the ways those words have influenced me.

Forget about marrying a doctor or lawyer, become one

My grandma Isabel (Mom's mother) graduated from college with a teaching credential and went on to become a teacher in public schools, traversing all the typical barriers of her time. She was young, a woman, and a Latina. She taught in a tiny one-room school many miles from home in a rural area of southern Colorado. She took her youngest daughter (Aunt Eleanor) with her and stayed next door to the school during the week, coming home on weekends. How she was ever allowed such an accomplishment is a still a mystery to me.

Grandma Isabel sounds like Laura's mom, "Forget about marrying a doctor or lawyer, become one." While she was alive, Grandma's tenacity served as a role model to my mom, even as she risked the criticism of the community to for not staying in her appropriate place in society. She instilled a yearning in my mom to go to college; however, Grandma's premature death squelched Mom's dream for decades. I celebrate that Mom spent twenty years in the classroom during the "encore" years of her life! —Linda

I know you wanted for us to be free from financial worries. Perhaps this is every mother's dream, especially those who come from homes and lineages where the line is thin between security and scarcity. What was it that made you so scared about having enough that it found its way into every conversation? How this fear lived in me for too long, twisting itself into a belief that every need is an act of selfishness and every request a burden. With my adult ears I can now hear in your letter the desire to be close to me, but as a teenager all I could sense was your anger, and all I could feel was guilt. Along with a strange impulse to stay near you, and at the same time, run away.

From the perspective of intergenerational trauma, a family member may take up an emotion or behavior on behalf of another family member who they sense cannot bear it,* thereby reducing trouble in the home. Perhaps in order to survive, neither you nor Grandma had patience with tender emotions like sadness. It seems my offering to our family was to absorb the emotions the rest of you could not afford to feel. I took them up as constant companions that I tried to metabolize, but they always seem to burst forth from my body at inopportune times.

---

a family member may take up an emotion or behavior on behalf of another family member who they sense cannot bear it

Role assignments often begin very early—whether given or self-assigned. Some family members are given permission to be fragile because of particular life circumstances, such as health conditions or life traumas. Because my mother had been orphaned, my father regarded her as someone who needed to be

> taken care of. For years, our family system operated in ways that centered on Dad's self-assigned role of caregiver and protector, and Mom's accepted role as the fragile one in need of care. To varying degrees, my brothers and I supported Dad's behavior as caregiver of Mom. Eventually, Mom clearly indicated how not-fragile she was. By then, we were fully operating in our caregiver roles. She had to assert herself to express her power. When she had truly become fragile, she truly needed us; my brothers and I had to adjust once more. This left me sad and scared. —Cari

I remember as a child when I wanted to hug you or jump in your lap out of delight, being pushed away, or alternatively when I would cry out to be soothed, feel you tense up as I came near. What happened to our people that made it so uncomfortable for you or Grandma to express warmth?

I know now as a therapist, when there has been a buildup of emotional pain, perhaps over generations, such feelings are a threat to the gated musculature protecting the heart. Now I understand that such coolness does not mean love isn't there; it just needed to be tucked away deep inside, erupting only when the anguish is so great it can't be contained. Like a great storm overwhelming a dam, each death in our family briefly threw open a window, affording a glimpse into how much we really meant to each other. When you died, Grandma's agony was so great it broke through her unsentimental veneer. At your funeral, she wailed deep and long, leaping onto your coffin and crying out for you, eventually having to be pulled off where she collapsed into a chair, inconsolable. I felt at the same instant horrified and relieved as she let out in one long wave a grief the rest of us were desperately attempting to swallow.

As your illness progressed, I continued to find ways to tuck away parts of myself that felt too threatening to our fragile familial composure. It seemed impossible for me to be an angry teenager with you so weak and suffering. There was no room for me to connect to my rage, a rage at you dying, a rage at the inevitable loss of the possibility you could ever become the mother I always longed for. My rage went underground and got acted out away from the family gaze. It also got bottled and shaped into a more acceptable form. If it began to bubble up when I was with you or Dad, I withdrew until I could return and present a more compliant version of myself.

I could sense you were an ambivalent mom, and I in turn became an ambivalent daughter. This only got worse after you got sick just as I was getting ready to start college. Facing all the grief of our family's situation with no support or anyone to talk to was too much for me. I found a therapist, and he offered me the permission I longed for to stay at college for the summer. At eighteen, I wanted to be in the world of the living, not the dying. I will never forget calling you on Mother's Day to let you know that I had decided I was going to stay at school that summer. I anxiously explained to you how I would be able to get a job and support myself so you wouldn't have to worry about the cost of me staying. I don't remember your exact response, but the sadness and disappointment in your voice was clear. That Mother's Day was the last time we spoke before you died. It took decades for me to untangle the guilt I carry over this moment, imagining what you must have felt when I chose to run away rather than face your leaving us. It continues to break my heart to the core; I am not sure I can ever get over these being the words I last spoke to you.

This therapist also encouraged me to write you and share everything I was feeling about you and your illness. I have forgotten so many details of my life then, but the card I wrote you not long before you died is seared in my memory. I stood in front of the pharmacy aisle for an inordinate amount of time struggling to choose which card to pick, as there is no "for my dying mother" Hallmark card section. I imagined that if I chose wisely the card might act as a talisman, bringing you closer to me. I was clinging to some subconscious fantasy of you reading the card and being so moved you would come running to me, taking me in your arms and expressing your love for me over and over, like a made-for-television movie.

Inside the card I let you know how much I loved and needed you, how I wanted you to find the strength to fight the cancer so you wouldn't die. Much more than that I can't remember now. I just know I didn't hold back. It felt terrifying and liberating to write. I waited for your response to my words, but they never arrived. Why, Mom, didn't you answer me?

What I didn't realize at the time is how much consolation that card would offer me after you died. What a relief I had let you know how much you meant to me.

I carried this lesson about grieving with me. When my sisters were dying, both in their early forties just like you, I could find a way to move towards them as their illnesses worsened, rather than away from them. With both Debbie and Janet, I was able to have at least one moment when the patterned familial boundaries between us felt more like a translucent veil that I could step through and share the depth of my heart before they were gone. By the time Dad died several years later, I felt as if I understood how to navigate the relational dance between those dying and those being left behind. I could appreciate all the unspoken, subtle, and even humorous ways he showed his love for me as his illness progressed. And in turn, I used any opportunity I could find to hug and speak my love for him. This included a letter offering what I hoped would be a comfort for a father leaving his last living daughter behind. I detailed with gratitude all he had given me and how, because of those gifts, I would be okay. And I am, for gratitude is the potential gift of knowing death.

Mom, I imagine if only you had a chance to live longer, we might have found a way to navigate love and loss in such an intimate way, instead of through silence, despair, and distance. After all this time, I still yearn for what can never be, and yet in that there is a relief to know that even after forty years my heart has not stopped wanting you.

Love,
Laura

~

(Thurs.) Feb. 11, 1982
Dear Laura,

I hope you are relaxing more. You worry too much about everything (like me). Now you are not only worrying about yourself but your boyfriend and Debbie too. You also rush too much like your father for no reason. We should be an example to you, nothing is more important than your health. Anything else can be overcome or changed. It was nice having you home for the week. Please keep writing me.

Mom

April 2020
Dear Mom,

I smile when I read your observation of me as this has been the same compassionate reflection from my husband, my Zen elders, and what I have observed of myself living in spiritual community. Yes, I am my father's daughter, inheriting his tendency to anxiously attend to others and to my surroundings with the hope that if all seems well on the outside, then perhaps I can be okay on the inside.

Being in constant attentive motion also helped me to keep floating above the seemingly bottomless well of heavy sadness I sunk into whenever I stopped, an unmetabolized grief I suspected was not mine alone but all of ours.

A few years after you died, some underground force drove me to find a way to heal what felt broken inside. Some mothering medicine to help complete what was only half born with you leaving too soon. A search for a wisdom that could make sense of loss. Your death prevented me from seeing life through the eyes of possibility alone, carrying at a young age a body knowing that I and everyone I care about will die.

Over the years I had to be taught how to decipher and give voice to the stirrings inside of me. I had to be taught how to dream and how to tolerate the risk of intimacy. How to deeply trust life as it has come to be, whether it shows up in the form of sorrow or joy, beginnings or endings.

Only in writing to you now did it dawn on me that you too were in pain and grieving. It is shocking that this is a revelation for me. How peculiar that despite all my years as a therapist and as a mentor to others in spiritual community, that until this moment, I had not allowed myself to consider that you too were navigating loss. Behind your words I can now sense into how lonely you must have been, how hard it was for you to have me so far away just as your illness was limiting your life in so many painful ways. How could I ever begin to understand what it was like for you to face death at forty-two, with so much life left unlived, leaving behind three young girls and not knowing what they would become? It's unimaginable. If someone in your situation walked into my therapy office or came to meet with me for spiritual guidance, how would I respond? Having walked with others through this, I know any spiritual truism cannot touch the depth of what an imminent death forces us to confront.

The summer before you died, you briefly went to a group for cancer survivors and their families. Dad refused to join you, and once you asked me to go with you, but I was too scared. Looking back, how could I have turned down a request to be with you in this way? What would I have learned about your grief had I the courage to have gone? I was such a terrified young woman; I am so sorry I missed this chance you offered me.

I can only imagine how vulnerable it was for you to enter into such a space. It makes me wonder now how that child too scared to be with that kind of pain influenced the woman I am today, my vocation creating space for what needs to be felt and named.

I read that those who lose their mothers young often try to honor their mothers' unfulfilled desires, as if we can somehow give them the years and lives they never got to live. At thirty I was on the brink of walking down a well-trodden path of marriage, complete with a house in the suburbs and motherhood. Instead, I took a sharp left turn and blew up my life. While this act appeared random and irresponsible to others, I was like a dog running around the yard, my restless heart following a scent beneath the ground, of which I wouldn't let go. I don't know what your unfulfilled desires were, but I sensed them as having a breadth of existence wider than the dimensions of our family's split-level tract home.

Yet our psyches are complicated and our lived experience never so straightforward and neat. I did want what was taken from me and from you. Some current beneath my awareness was guiding me. I wanted home and I wanted family, just not in the form I had been given.

I found my way to the mothering energy I needed, or perhaps it found me. It came to me from therapists, through a few devoted female friends. It came to me through my husband, who taught me how to trust love by his unwavering commitment to me. It came to me through my Zen teachers, who took my aspiration to live fully and deeply seriously, who taught me how to sit in the middle of suffering and find peace and ease. It came to me in the silence of being in the forests and swimming in the lake. It whispered words of love, of belonging, of forgiveness. I imagined it as your voice speaking to me with the land quieting me so I could hear you.

For the last fifteen years, I have been bringing mothering energy to others as a therapist, Buddhist teacher, and devoted parent to two dogs. My home is now a monastery. Each day, we wake up, sit, cook, eat, cry, study, struggle, and laugh together. I find myself at times, like you, worrying about keeping this "household" going and occasionally feeling overwhelmed by my aspiration to spend this life devoted to caring for the well-being of others. But mostly I feel contentment living simply in community.

My spiritual practice has offered me a place to care for my grief. My grief is held in the beauty of ritual: I bring it to my meditation cushion; I offer it over to my spiritual ancestors as I bow and chant, helping me to realize I am forever embedded in a web of relationships extending in all directions. My grief is held in communal arms that understand it as worthy of respect and care. It is spoken with a recognition that this is how life is. We are always in a process of grieving. Life is always slipping out of our hands, returning in the next moment into a new form. Without death, there would be no possibility for life. I live now in the midst of trees and rivers and many other nonhuman beings who remind me each day that death is the natural way of things, not just some personal tragic tale of loss.

I no longer think that grief is something I need to get over; its medicine brings me into a more grateful relationship to all of life. I welcome my capacity to grieve. To be able to appreciate, as you taught me, the gift of health and to choose wisely, knowing how precious and fleeting this all is.

Mom, I hope I never stop grieving you, for it is how my love for you lives in me and honors what we lost. I won't stop speaking with you. Even though you can't respond in kind, writing you has helped my grief to settle into a sweet tenderness and recognition of the ongoing depth of our connection.

I love you,
Laura

∼

August 2020
Dearest Mom,

My family now includes all the Buddhist ancestors who offer me wise guidance in navigating life's hardships, losing you being the hardest. I wanted to share with you this poem inspired by one of the first women who practiced in a lineage I call home. Written by a mother grieving her dead daughter, it speaks equally to me as a daughter, mourning the loss of a mother. Falling to the ground in surrender to my anguish at your death, I find lying next to me all those who have deeply loved and deeply lost. Their comforting presence mysteriously allows me to hear you again. I'll be forever listening for your voice calling back.

All my love,
Laura

A Voice Calling Back

UBBIRI ~ THE EARTH[2]

How many days and nights
did I wander the woods
calling your name?

Jiva, my daughter!

Jiva, my heart!

Late one night,
finally exhausted,
I fell to the ground.

Oh, my heart, I heard a voice say,

*84,000 daughters all named Jiva
have died and been buried
here in this boundless cemetery
you call a world.*

For which of these Jivas are you mourning?

Lying there on the ground,
I shared my grief with those 84,000 mothers.

And they shared their grief with me.

Somehow I found myself healed—
not of grief,
but of the immeasurable loneliness
that attends grief.

My sisters.
Those of you who have known the deepest
   loss.

As you cry out in the wilderness,
just make sure
you stop
every so often
to listen for a voice calling back.

---

2. Weingast, *The First Free Women*, 41–42. "The Earth" is a poetic interpretation of a poem written by the early Buddhist nun Ubbiri. Ubbiri's original poem is found in the ancient Buddhist text the Therēgāthā, which is considered to be the world's oldest collection of women's literature in India.

PART II: GRIEVING

QUESTIONS FOR REFLECTION

1. What formal or informal rituals were available for your mourning process after the death of a loved one? What did those rituals offer you at the time?

2. What, if any, are the rituals you still engage in to keep you connected to those you have lost?

3. How might you open up and further the story of your relationship with those who have died?

4. Is there something still hurting around your relationship with a deceased family member? What can you bring to that experience now that might allow it to further heal?

6

Fragmented Souvenir
Witnessing a Life

SU YON PAK

STANDING IN OUR PARENTS' apartment, my sister and I are surveying the enormity of the move that will need to happen quickly. Every nook and cranny is filled with items that span the years of their lives. Some items, like yards and yards of embroidered silk tablecloths, are the originals that came in a shipping crate from South Korea when we immigrated in 1971. Many other items have been acquired over the years, like a large electric pressure cooker that made their favorite seven-grain bean rice, or the restaurant-size metal bowl with dents from frequent use that can hold a whole box of napa cabbage for making kimchi. Looking around, we marvel at our father's handiwork: the extra shelves and makeshift clothes closets that not only increased the holding capacity of their home but created a logical system that only the two of them shared. Overwhelmed at the task of re/organizing our parents' lives without their guidance, we create our own logical system—anything that can be easily replaced will be thrown out.

My mother had just been diagnosed with Alzheimer's disease. Several years of more-than-usual worrisome forgetfulness eventually culminated in a frightening episode that led to her hospitalization. After a series of transpacific family meetings, our siblings and I made a decision to move our parents closer to us to facilitate the care of our mother. It would be a major move, from Long Island, where they had lived for over thirty years, to Westchester, where they had their occasional holiday visits to their daughters. It would mean leaving their network of church community, friends, and my mother's siblings, with whom they had monthly gatherings. Because the move would disorient and agitate our mother further, we sent our parents on a "vacation" to our other sister's house in North Carolina while we cleaned out their apartment for sale. In order to fit all their life possessions into a small one-bedroom apartment at a senior living facility, we dedicated every weekend for over a month to cleaning, discarding, packing, and repeating—until, finally, we gave in and called a "junk" removal service and paid them, pleaded with them, to take away their things.

Emotionally, it was relatively painless for us to clear out a closet full of clothes (many still with price tags attached), drawers full of kitchen gadgets, a storage cage full of seventy empty kimchi jars, suitcases, and portable heaters that no longer worked, among many other random items. But it was a display cabinet of my mother's cherished souvenirs that caused unexpected anxiety for me. Objects from Jerusalem, Mexico, Afghanistan, and other faraway places held a place of honor in that display cabinet. These objects were not of much use in my parents' daily life—the teaspoon with the Canadian maple leaf, which was too small for tea; a contraption that looked like a hookah pipe from Turkey, which sat there collecting oil and dust; the Seder plate from Jerusalem, which held their unwanted mail; and the Caithness glass paper weight from Scotland, which was moved from place to place to make room for other objects.

The irony is that these souvenirs did not perform the function for which they were created, namely, to assist my parents "to come to mind" of the places from which these objects came. "To come to mind" is the Old French verb form of the noun souvenir from the Latin *subvenire*, which means "come to mind"—from *sub*, "up from below."[1] In fact, my parents had never been in these places. Their friends and family had given them these objects as mementos of their travels. Though I am guilty of doing the same, this practice of bringing souvenirs back to people who have never visited a place seems rather curious. I am not sure what is supposed to "come to mind" while gazing at these objects, except that the recipients were thought of. Still, disposing of these objects felt like I was throwing

---

1. For full etymology of souvenir, see: https://www.etymonline.com/word/souvenir.

away some cherished memories of my parents, who might have imbued each object with an essence of the person who gave it.

But then, probably not. My parents no longer remembered who gave them these souvenirs, nor did they remember the occasions on which these gifts were received. And yet these "useless" objects held certain indiscernible meaning for my mother. She had held onto them even through several downsizing efforts. Or perhaps, just like the seventy empty kimchi jars, these objects were still there because they could not part with them, in case, just in case, they needed them. Like many Koreans of their generation, perhaps it was performative memory rooted in war, dislocation, and trauma.

As I reflect on caring for my mother for a decade in varying degrees of capacities and intensities, souvenirs serve as a metaphor to explore the complex and textured relationship between memory, identity, trauma, and loss. As a metaphor, my mother's souvenirs go beyond the materiality of mementos externalized as objects; they are internal markers that guide the topography of her life.* The internal markers present themselves as stories told, secrets held, everyday practices interrupted or lived, and traumas re/enacted. These markers play out both in the personal and in the sociohistorical, geopolitical domains. My mother's personal memory is inextricably tied to major historical events. Whether her souvenirs are stories of her childhood under Japanese colonization when she was forced to learn Japanese as her "stepmother" tongue, or when she was compelled to leave her ancestral home (crossing the thirty-eighth parallel from the north to the southern part of Korea), or her experience as a nurse during the Korean War, all are her memories—written, erased, and written over—that create a palimpsest* of a personal and political living human document.[2] Traces of previous memories that had been erased to make space for new ones still appear like ghostly reminders of the past, haunting the present.

internal markers that guide the topography of her life

I am particularly drawn to Su's understanding of externalized objects used as internal markers. Thanks to Su for helping me understand more fully one of my mom's strange dementia-induced behaviors—affixing her address labels on multiple things

2. Anton Boisen, the founder of clinical pastoral education, believed that the study of human experience, "reading" the living human document, was crucial for theological training to complement classroom learning.

other than mailing envelopes. When I realized Mom couldn't remember phone numbers anymore and had difficulty using her personal address book and telephone diary, I created a simplified list of phone numbers of key people she often called, and taped the list on the wall near her phone. Mom affixed address labels onto this list, saying she felt the address labels would secure the list better. Then she affixed a label in each of her purses, saying that if she were injured while out of her home, whoever would help her could identify who she was fairly easily. When she began affixing the labels to some of her clothes, she said this was to affirm that she had not stolen what she was wearing. While I knew this behavior was brought on by her dementia, thanks to Su, I now understand that Mom was using these labels to remind herself of who she was. —Cari

---

a palimpsest

A palimpsest reminds me of the theory of *pentimento*, which is a term used in art. Pentimento describes how an old painting that is covered over seeps through the new piece of art that is painted on the same canvas. It sometimes describes what happens when an artist changes his or her mind and paints over an old artwork, and the pentimento energizes the artist to create a new piece of art that takes into account both what was there before and what is here now. What if we used the theory of pentimento when we think of our own lives—if we used this to describe the rootedness in ourselves and discover how this old painting can be made into a new piece of art?

Su's reference to the palimpsest also reminds me of the ways my family told stories about their experiences from generation to generation. The memories of trauma, isolation, and oppression made space for learning, tenacious recovery, and changing course. Unfortunately, many of these stories were not written or recorded, so we cling to our memories passed down through a rich oral tradition, which I liken to the "third space" that Su describes. —Linda

This chapter is an exploratory foray into the complex web of grief *and* blessing I experienced as I cared for my mother. Her memory loss both animated *and* disrupted the life she had lived under the long shadow of historical and personal trauma. The slow but progressive loss of function and the self as she knew it meant that the loss of my mother was ambiguous[3]—without a clear or definite end. What lurked behind the hazy forgetting were the stark

---

3. Boss, *Ambiguous Loss*.

remembrances of the past. She moved in and out of various ages of her life, at times like they were the present, and at other times, like they were ghostly hauntings.[4] What was lost was not gone but remained to haunt and disrupt the normative ways of seeing and being. What was forgotten was concealed just beneath the surface to be brought up to mind (*subvenire*). Drawing on Johannes Metz's concept of "dangerous memory," I problematize the binary relationship between remembering and forgetting, in particular, what I call "dangerous amnesia." Dangerous memory and dangerous amnesia are co-constitutive and create what Homi Bhabha calls a "third space,"[5] where my mother often lived with her Alzheimer's—a space that destabilizes linear and binary distinctions of time, memory, identity, order, and relationships.

PAST STILL PRESENT: FAILED REMEMBERING AND INCOMPLETE FORGETTING

Caring for my mother who had Alzheimer's was a practice in assembling a jigsaw puzzle with no guiding image. I had to study the cut out pieces with their holes and knobs, interlocking them piece by piece observing the picture that was emerging. Unlike the jigsaw puzzle with its unique pieces, the caring puzzle I was putting together had many pieces that could be interchanged with others. And depending on the combination of pieces, a different picture would emerge. Caring for my mother was like assembling puzzle pieces hoping that I had the correct combination so that I could minimize harm in the process. Ensuring that her physical, emotional, social, and spiritual needs were attended to became more of a challenge as she lost the ability to assess and communicate her needs. But what was even more trying was the relational piece of the puzzle. As a daughter who has had an attentive relationship with her mother, my daily interactions had the comfort of well-worn tracks on a familiar relational terrain. I had an intertwining history with shared narratives and memories that formed and informed who *I* was and who *she* was. I was a daughter because she was my mother. Daughter and mother are relational identities. They function only in relation to the other. As I wrote elsewhere,

---

4. Gordon, *Ghostly Matters*.

5. Bhabha, *The Location of Culture*. "Third Space" for Bhabha, is the liminal space where cultures collide and give rise to different representations and meanings. This is an "in-between" space where new identities are re/formed and are becoming. Also see Rutherford, "The Third Space," 207–21.

Part II: Grieving

> Shared memories, the hyphen between mother—daughter,
> Broken...
>
> Can daughter exist when mother does not?
> Dangling as a participle searching for the subject to modify.
> Dangling...[6]

As my mother's Alzheimer's progressed and her ability to remember declined, she forgot not only what she did, but who she was. In particular, my mother's "mother-identity" eroded away, piece by piece, unilaterally robbing me of my "daughter-identity." This interlocking relationship, dismantled and built, dismantled again and built again, gave way to a loss that was ambiguous, incomplete, and uncertain, leaving me and my mother with ambiguous nonconforming identities. She was still my mother, but not my mother. She was still there but was not there. She continually said goodbye without leaving. And she left without saying goodbye. It was an unending loss that came in small increments over an extended period of time. My desire for certainty and closure often led to feelings of guilt for even having such desires. Pauline Boss observes that these uncertain movements of loss prevent people from renegotiating the roles and rules of their relationship with the loved one. They remain stuck in the dynamics and identities of their previous known relationship.[7] While this concept of ambiguous loss was helpful as it gave voice to what was happening, naming it a "loss" did not entirely capture my experience. Yes, it was a loss. At the same time, the ambiguity of the loss opened up space for the "gain" and the "find," however incomplete and tenuous those gains and finds were. Precisely because it was not final, there was space for possibilities. Namely, rather than being "frozen in place," [8] I was responding to her change by shifting my roles and the rules of my relationship with my mother. I found myself entering her world* rather than demanding her to be in mine.

> Contemplating radical love, I enter her world
> a world of ghosts, war and ancestors that terrifies me.
>
> With love's rope tied around my waist, I enter her holy of holies.
> The other end of the rope, tethered firmly to this world.[9]

---

6. Pak, "Contemplating Radical Love."
7. Boss, *Ambiguous Loss*, 7.
8. Boss, *Ambiguous Loss*, 7.
9. Pak, "Contemplating Radical Love."

entering her world

I am moved by Su's capacity to witness and absorb all of what her mom was trying to share with her life—through her notebooks, through the objects in her home, through her reliving the past in the present, through her ways of relating to those around her; by Su stepping back and attentively listening to what her mom was expressing and not expressing, hearing the memory fragments, pieces of trauma too unbearable for her to carry around in explicit memory. I'm impressed by Su being able to let go enough of the mom she knew and being willing to time travel with her so she could receive the survival knowledge in her mom's "dangerous memories," the intergenerational experiences carried to one's offspring. Her writing illuminates that who our mothers were and who we are as daughters is not a static story but a continual unfolding that asks us not to grasp any descriptions we offer as a final truth.

After death, it can be so tempting to freeze our mother/daughter stories in time and not allow new narratives to emerge, to not allow ourselves to consider, as Su writes, "what we forget and what we discard." In reading and rereading my mother's few letters to me, I had to quiet down the desperate daughter inside in order to listen for the woman who was writing to me. While the fragments of our relationship are still painfully sparse, I now have faith she will continue to disclose her life to me if I can be a willing and loving witness to a presence which survives death.
—Laura

The ambiguity was daring me to create new narratives, to try out different roles and to puzzle together unlikely pieces. The relationship with my mother was in a dynamic dance of perpetual negotiations with energy and curiosity that revealed insights about my mother, myself, and our shared stories.

These insights are not just personal; they also hold subversive sociopolitical "dangerous memory." Johannes Metz proposes that for memory to have the power to transform society, it has to be dangerous. For Metz, memory is not some passive, nostalgic exercise in recall.* Memory is not a "middle-class counterpart to hope, leading us deceptively away from the risks of the future."[10] Rather, dangerous memory is an active memory of suffering and freedom, that makes demands on us. It has the subversive power to break through the prevailing, normative structures. "Such

---

10. Metz, *Faith in History and Society*, 109.

memories are like dangerous and incalculable visitations from the past."[11] They are memories with a *future* content.

---

memory is not some passive, nostalgic exercise in recall

When Mom no longer remembered the job Dad had had for thirty-four years, it was disorienting for my brothers and me.

In 1955, Dad became the first Black mail carrier in his postal district, serving in an upper-income white community. Mom awakened at 4 a.m. to wake him up, packed his lunch every workday, and greeted him with kisses and hugs upon his return home from work, especially to provide emotional support and encouragement to Dad as he dealt with intense racism. So, when her dementia progressed to the point that she no longer recalled what job he had, we were shocked and didn't know how to process this new reality.

My brothers and I were caught in memory of Dad's work both as a nostalgic exercise in recall and as a source of pride for how he withstood racism. Because of dementia, Mom had released the need for nostalgia, pride, and anger. She was no longer attached to the things that had been important to her except for two things: giving and receiving love, and relying upon and thanking God.

Whether or not Mom remembered knowing someone, she expressed unconditional love to them. Whether or not she remembered the song lyrics of her favorite hymns, she sang praises to God. Whether she was eating in a fine restaurant or eating puréed food in the nursing home, she expressed profound delight and gratitude. In this way, Mom's forgetting was instructive and liberatory for me.

Su also writes, "forgetting led to remembering and remembering led to forgetting." By forgetting the things in her life that she had grown attached to, my Mom remembered a deeper capacity for freedom and love. By remembering and embracing freedom and love, she forgot the pain of being abandoned by her mother and father. —Cari

---

Visitations from the past, or perhaps more accurately visitations *to* the past, were regular occurrences for my mother as she struggled with the confusion of disordered time, events, and reality. She could not remember what she ate for dinner or whether she ate a meal at all. She could not remember how to knit, an activity she had done with great passion and

---

11. Metz, *Faith in History and Society*, 109–10.

expertise for over sixty years. Nor did she remember that she needed to wait till her red nail polish dried before rubbing her hands together. The hymns she learned from American missionaries, like "Softly and Tenderly Jesus Is Calling" which she used to sing almost daily, in English, off-key but with gusto, were no longer in her spiritual lexicon. She no longer remembered the words; instead, she sang in Japanese, the forbidden Japanese military songs she was forced to learn as a child under the Japanese occupation. She did not remember that her husband of over fifty years had passed. In fact, she did not remember my father being in any constellation of her family. Her family consisted of her unique family of origin—namely, her siblings, her parents (whom she resurrected), and me (whom she sometimes called her sister, when asked). I became both her *ddal* and *unni*, her daughter and her older sister. I was her daughter whom she gave birth to, and her older sister who remained with her husband's family in what is now North Korea when my mother's family crossed over the thirty-eighth parallel. Actually, on certain days, my mother was still there in North Korea, and on other days she was in South Korea as a nursing student, nursing wounded enemy soldiers during the Korean War.

For my mother, this *endangered* memory, threatened with extinction, became a *dangerous* memory. This dangerous memory, which broke through from the past to the present and future, revealed "new and dangerous insights for the present."[12] Her Alzheimer's-induced reality persistently exposed the current reality of this unending Korean War. There was no peace treaty. The division of the Korean Peninsula continues to this day, almost seventy years after the ceasefire—the Korean Armistice Agreement of July 27, 1953. In case we forget, in case the world forgets, her dangerous memory betrayed the lie that the semblance of "peace" on the Korean Peninsula was, in essence, not peace, but "the face of a 'war without end.'"[13] Through her Alzheimer's-induced reality, she actively lived this war in the present, demanding that we remember that this war has not ended. My mother, who was forgetting the present, was reminding us of that past, which was, in fact, still present.

Yet, as Grace Cho reminds us, "this place is neither an origin nor a final destination." This ghostly state kept my mother "suspended between

---

12. Metz, *Faith in History and Society*, 109.

13. Christine Hong cites Achille Mbembe, "Necropolitics," trans. Libby Meintjes, *Public Culture* 15.1 (2003) 23, in "The Unending Korean War," in *Positions: Asia Critique* 23.4 (Nov 2015).

Part II: Grieving

a failed remembering and an incomplete forgetting."[14] While rummaging for (lost) memories in that suspended place, she found the hauntings of recovered memories. My mother's recovered memories that traversed the time-space continuum, and not linearly or chronologically, took her to her childhood in northern Korea, picking ripe plums for her brother to eat. The failed remembering and incomplete forgetting of the ancestral home she left behind in North Korea, and the divided peninsula with families separated on both sides, were both present and not present. It was not accessible to her though it was still there.* Her sister left behind in North Korea was there and not there. She had heard from her from time to time, but she was no longer accessible to her. Suspended between what was present and not present, my mother was haunted by the ghost that makes itself known through its own logic and cognition. As Avery Gordon explains:

> The ghost or the apparition is one form by which something lost, or barely visible, or seemingly not there to our supposedly well-trained eyes, makes itself known or apparent to us, in its own way, of course. The way of the ghost is haunting, and haunting is a very particular way of knowing what has happened or is happening. Being haunted draws us affectively, sometimes against our will and always a bit magically, into the structure of feeling of a reality we come to experience, not as cold knowledge but as a transformative recognition.[15]

Her sister left behind in North Korea was there and not there

Joy Bokshin Lee Gebhard was fifteen years old when she left Pyongyang, North Korea, for Seoul with other refugees on December 3, 1950. Her mother stayed behind to keep the family property. She was wearing her school uniform with additional layers of clothing, carrying rice and snacks her mother packed for her. She somehow knew that she would not see her mother again. This poem is her story. —Su

---

14. Cho, *Haunting the Korean Diaspora*, 79.
15. Gordon, *Ghostly Matters*, 8.

FRAGMENTED SOUVENIR

We Never Said Goodbye[16]
By Joy Bokshin Lee Gebhard

I cry in night as I see my mother in my dream
She welcomes me and says,
'So you are home
You have been away for so long'—
I cry in night in my dream
for I couldn't reach my mother

As I awake,
it was just a dream
still I go home every night
though my home is beyond the 38 Parallel
I miss seeing my sisters and brother playing in the garden
and the ducklings swimming in the pond
I miss my mother—to whom
I never said goodbye

She said softly as I was leaving:
'write often,
Seoul is cold ...
keep warm
stay alive'

She stood long by the gate watching me leaving

We never said good bye
We never said good bye

Re/membering long-term memories as a result of my mother's loss of short-term memory is like following the ghost. It is like breathing life into and enfleshing the ghost "where only a vague memory or a bare trace was visible."[17] My mother's re/membered stories brought the erased writings of the palimpsest into sharp relief even as the current memories were left in the shadowy manifestations of amnesia.

This ghostly world disrupts the binary categories of remembering and forgetting, memory and amnesia. In considering memory, and more specifically, dangerous memory, we need to also consider forgetting, or what I call dangerous amnesia. If there is dangerous remembering, isn't there also dangerous forgetting?* If we examine what we remember and what we hold on to, should we not also examine what we forget and what we discard?

16. Joy Bokshin Lee Gebhard shared her story at the 70 Years of the Korean War: Intergenerational Korean American Women's Dialogue and Virtual Vigil on July 23, 2020, hosted by Korea Peace Network, Korea Peace Now! Grassroots Network, and Peace Treaty Now. Read her interview: Jung, "Separated Families Cry Out."

17. Gordon, *Ghostly Matters*, 22.

Part II: Grieving

dangerous forgetting

What is the distinction between dangerous forgetting that disempowers and dangerous forgetting that empowers? In the first instance it functions as repression and denial and thus cuts us off from life. In the second instance it lets go of oppressive constructs that prevent a full and inclusive expression of humanness.

There is a dangerous forgetting imposed on minoritized groups in society who are different from what is considered to be normal. More importantly, there is a dangerous forgetting of transgression in the name of justice and greater inclusivity. This is the dangerous forgetting of queerness. When we queer a norm, we are looking to forget—with subversive intent—all that was disciplined into us regarding what "normal" gender and sexuality expression were supposed to be in order to express its authenticity in our lives.

The dangerous forgetting of mourning the loss of our mothers exists in this contradiction. When we mourn, we allow ourselves to feel the loss of an established norm; that is, we are now motherless in a world that sees the presence of biological mothers as normal. At the same time, we are free to create a subversive new normal that expresses the many possible ways we experience a mother in our lives. For some it might be embracing an older sister, an aunt, or grandmother. For others it might be important women from outside the family of origin who become our mothers. And for others it might be the nurturing men who mother us. While we embrace the memory of our deceased mother, we learn to embrace a new mother who grounds us as we move through life. Mourning the loss of a mother, then, creates the possibility of constructing a nonnormative family—a queer family. —Kathy

As a society, we tend to valorize enterprises that produce and keep memory, such as museums, libraries, monuments, war memorials, memory market technology, and the greeting card and souvenir industries. These enterprises ensure that we keep and remember what we deem of value, what we must not forget. But to keep the "valuable" memories "sacred," the society discards unwanted "profane" memories to keep them away, to be forgotten. In particular, the memory-producing enterprises have their counterparts in amnesia-producing enterprises, like trash, landfills, e-waste dumping sites,[18] mass graves, prisons, and Alzheimer's. However, these amnesia-producing spaces, which I contend are ghostly spaces, are

---

18. CNN reports that China is the world's largest e-waste dumping site. See Watson, "China."

not simply places of discarding and forgetting. These spaces are powerful, subversive spaces that disrupt the fixed binary construction of memory and amnesia. They offer the potential to blur the existing boundaries, to make space for new meanings to arise. They are liminal or in-between spaces where translations and negotiations happen. They are instances of what Homi Bhabha calls "third space."[19]

Caring for my mother with progressing Alzheimer's and negotiating and translating her world to mine was very often an experience of this "third space." Her life of continual displacement—Japanese occupation, multiple wars, migration as a refugee, and immigration to the US—was capped by my mother's final displacement through Alzheimer's. Her final displacement demanded a different paradigm around remembering and forgetting. When I entered her Alzheimer's-induced world, I encountered a world not limited by socially constructed conventions of time and space, a world where social relationships were unhinged and reordered, a world where ghosts became flesh and flesh became ghosts, and a world where the time of war and the time of healing coexisted synchronously. I was entering a third space* with its own time, logic, and language. It was a space with the possibility of a *home* she so longed for all her life.

---

entering a third space

I introduce a song of this in-between, "third space" called *The Thunder: Perfect Mind*. It is an ancient poem from Nag Hamadi, thought to have been used by Egyptian Christians that dates back as early as the first century BCE and as late as the third century CE. Lost and forgotten for many centuries, *Thunder* is a ghostly speech written mostly in feminine voice. As a series of divinely proclaimed "I am" statements, it disrupts socially constructed categories and binaries around identity, gender, and relations.[20] It is a language of a "third space" my mother inhabited. —Su

> The Thunder: Perfect Mind
> (1:5–9, 1:3–4, 4:14–15, 2:1–2)[21]
>
> I am the first and the last
> I am she who is honored and she who is mocked

---

19. Bhabha, *The Location of Culture*, 55.
20. Taussig et al., trans., *The Thunder*, 39.
21. Taussig, *A New New Testament*, 183, 185.

Part II: Grieving

I am the whore and the holy woman
I am the wife and the virgin
I am he the mother and the daughter
I am the limbs of my mother
I am a sterile woman and she has many children
I am she whose wedding is extravagant and I didn't have a husband.
I am the midwife and she who hasn't given birth
I am the comfort of my labor pains
I am the bride and the bridegroom
And it is my husband who gave birth to me
I am my father's mother,
My husband's sister, and he is my child

Don't chase me from your sight
Don't let your voice or your hearing hate me
Don't ignore me any place, any time
Be careful. Do not ignore me

I am peace and war exists because of me
I am a foreigner and a citizen of the city
I am being
I am she who is nothing

I am the silence never found
And the idea infinitely recalled
I am the voice with countless sounds
And the thousand guises of the word
I am the speaking of my name

HOME, A FRAGMENTED SOUVENIR

With her failing memory, my mother's desire for home intensified. It is as if "home" had become a mnemonic device—the souvenir—"to call to mind" the fading stories of her life. It became the central puzzle piece that oriented other fragmented pieces. Unlike nostalgic longings,[22] her homesickness was not remembering the home of her past filtered through fragmented memories that were pieced together. Rather, it was the future home she recalled

---

22. According to Tracey Benson, "Nostalgic desire, as opposed to other forms of desire, lies somewhere between resemblance and identity, because it is enamored by or attracted to substance—being the souvenir. The past is constructed and made whole by piecing together the remaining fragmented memories—there is no resemblance, no continuous identity beyond this existence" (Benson, "Museum of the Personal," 39).

and imagined for which she hoped and searched. It was a future-oriented physical location with certain attributes that only she could articulate. It was a homesickness with future content. This "homing" desire mirrored her own development as an elderly woman with Alzheimer's.

In his book *Dementia: Living in the Memories of God*, John Swinton challenges the common understanding of people with Alzheimer's as being like children. Because their short-term memory is lost and may be locked in a period of their lives when they were much younger, or maybe, because of loss of inhibition, they may act like children. But they are adults with a history and a story that make them who they are. Even if my mother could not hold on to her memories, "her body remain[ed] formed and available in a world which has bodily familiarity even if that familiarity can no longer be named."[23] My mother was not moving backward toward her childhood; she was moving forward toward her new future self. She was living in the past *and* living toward her future self. This insight interrupts the one-way motion of the linear time construct of past-present-future. It rearticulates temporal boundaries.

Years before my mother was formally diagnosed with Alzheimer's, she had a habit of writing and rewriting her life stories. This habit came naturally to her as one of her faithful spiritual practices was studying the Bible by copying the scriptures. She did this in Korean. And she did this in English. She believed that this was a way of praying the Scripture three times:* once with her eyes by reading, twice with her mouth as she quietly uttered the passages out loud, and thrice with her hand by committing them onto paper.

---

praying the Scripture three times

The notebook pages of stories that Su's mother wrote are awe-inspiring, as is the ways in which she arranged and apparently rearranged them as she wrote them over and over in her native Korean language. Su's description of the way in which her mother prayed the Scriptures also reveals her commitment to remembering. I rarely referenced the Bible until later in life when I converted to a Protestant tradition. What came as a surprise was how much easier it was for me to remember the content of the Scriptures if I studied them in Spanish, the language of my childhood, even though I forgot a lot as a result of assimilation. I have

---

23. Swinton, *Dementia*, 82–83.

Part II: Grieving

not prayed the Scripture in Su's mother's way, but am inspired to try the practice in Spanish. —Linda

My mother did the same with her life stories. In her ninety-nine-cent spiral notebooks that she kept safely in some dresser or box, she would fill every line and page with her scribbly Korean handwriting. From time to time, at family gatherings, she would bring out her notebooks and read us her stories, commanding me to translate them to our children and their generation. When we were cleaning out her apartment, I found her notebooks. Flipping through pages of her writing, I was struck by what I saw. She had written fragments of stories over and over again as if to "perfect" the story, or perhaps to "pray" the story. These pages were torn out from the notebooks, rearranged, stapled together in a different order. It was difficult to make heads or tails of where one story ended and another began. Multiple versions of the same story had numbered pages, but, looking at the paper texture and color, they were torn from different notebooks and stapled together. It was as if these fragments were souvenirs from temporal places she had visited and revisited in her memory. When I finally made some sense of the fragmented pages, four stories emerged. They were stories that marked the "boundary events"[24] of her life: stories of border crossings—both spatial and political. She even titled them: Day of Liberation, August 15, 1945; Crossing the thirty-eighth parallel—the second try; June 25, 1950, the day the Korean War broke out; and Remembering May 25, 1971 (the day we landed in the U.S. as immigrants).

Like the fragmented souvenirs of the places she had been to, these stories "called to mind" the self that was coming clearer into focus *because* of the self that was forgotten. As if all the stored memories were vying for her attention, forgetting led to remembering; and remembering led to forgetting. In her, dangerous memory and dangerous forgetting were co-constitutive.

---

24. Trinh, "Far Away, From Home." She writes about her home in this essay. I quote: "Today, when I'm asked where home is for me, I am struck by how far away it is; and yet, home is nowhere else but right here, at the edge of this body of mine" ("Far Away, From Home," 12). These multiple ways of "homing" is also about becoming a boundary event. Rather than breaking down walls or transcending boundaries, Trinh talks about being home in the boundary. In Gloria Anzaldúa's words, "This is her home/ this thin edge/ of barbwire." Anzaldúa, *Borderlands/La Frontera*, 13. Becoming a boundary event is about tuning the intervals between any twos, "constantly tread(ing) the fine line between positioning and de-positioning" (Far Away, From Home," 54).

Fragmented Souvenir

My mother's loss of memory brought back with vivid details the dangerous memories of the defining moments of her life. As I read her pieced-together writings of *yook-ee-oh* (6-2-5), June 25th 1950, I recalled the stories she would tell us repeatedly about that day. Her writing, her stories, her memories, and my memories became entwined as I continued to assemble the puzzle pieces of her life.* I could taste, smell, and hear the sounds of the war, fear, fury, and determination. She was back there—the day the Korean War broke out—back in Seoul, in her nursing school, as a third-year student, in her white uniform, blue apron, and white cap. Sounds of sirens, loudspeakers, and bombings. She was back there—the enemy tanks pointing their guns outside her nursing school, commanding people to surrender. She relived the anger, fear, and tears of fury as the enemy ordered them out to "greet" the injured enemy soldiers. She recalled being coaxed by her younger colleague, "*Unni*, don't cry. Don't show that you are crying. You will be in trouble. Go out there and smile to the enemy soldiers . . ." Resisting but complying, she swallowed her pride and rage, dried her tears, and greeted them. She vividly remembered nursing the wounds of enemy soldiers, sterilizing the equipment in Lysol. With her hand she closed the open eyes of dead soldiers while making her rounds. She quietly chanted the Florence Nightingale pledge like a talisman as she devoted herself to the welfare of those committed to her care whether they were friend or foe, urged on by a practice of her adopted Christian faith: "Love your enemies and pray for those who persecute you" (Matt 5:44 NRSV). This kind of remembering is like writing ghost stories. These enfleshed stories "not only repair representational mistakes, but also strive to understand the conditions under which a memory was produced in the first place, toward a countermemory, for the future."[25]

I continued to assemble the puzzle pieces of her life

I was fascinated by Su's narrative about her mother's notebooks and how, as Su made sense of the fragments, four stories emerged of "boundary events" from her mother's experiences as a refugee, as she crossed the border between North and South Korea and eventually into to the United States. I was so moved by Su's capacity to piece together the fragments and to theorize the complexity of how memory and forgetting interweave, especially as trauma is splintered by dementia.

---

25. Gordon, *Ghostly Matters*, 22.

Part II: Grieving

> Because my maternal grandmother never learned to speak English, and she never told my mother, who understood Yiddish, what had happened to her in Eastern Europe, I never heard a single story from either of them about what caused a terrified nineteen-year-old girl to flee for her life. I know I am not alone. Many people don't have even fragments of the stories of what happened to their parents, grandparents, and great-grandparents who survived (or didn't) oppression, enslavement, rape, torture, and war.
>
> What I do know is that my grandmother had blond hair and blue eyes. The only one in an extended family of dark-haired, dark-eyed, Semitic-looking people. Growing up I heard snide, knowing "jokes" about Cossacks.
>
> When I recently read Caroline Randall Williams's remarkable article "You Want a Confederate Monument? My Body is a Confederate Monument" in the Sunday June 26, 2020, edition of the *New York Times*, those "jokes" came rushing back to mind.[26] Reading this sentence—"I am a black, Southern woman, and of my immediate white male ancestors, all of them were rapists"—I shuddered at the impact of Caroline Williams's courage and the power of speaking her truth into the cacophony of noxious and shameful arguments against removal of monuments that honor those who fought against the United States to preserve their "right" to enslave Black people. I also shuddered at the recognition that I am likely only three generations removed from the rape of my great-grandmother, whose name I never even knew.
>
> There are the stories; there are the fragments; there is the forgetting; and then there is the storing of traumatic memory in bodies, which echoes through the centuries with deafening silence. —Bobbi

My mother was in the war, and she was here too, in her nursing home where she was busy "nursing" other residents back to health. She made her daily rounds, dropping into residents' rooms. She helped to feed residents who could not feed themselves. Every time I went to visit her, she marveled with a genuine surprise and delight, "How did you find me here? How did you know that I was here?" She would tell me that she was so busy that we could not spend too long doing our weekly ritual of getting her nails done or eating *mandoo* (Korean dumplings) at a nearby restaurant.

As I took her for an afternoon outing from the nursing home, she would call out to the nurses at the nursing station, "I'll be back. I am going out for just a bit." They would all nod knowingly. Then she would ask me furtively, "Did you ask for time off for me?"

26. See Williams, "You Want a Confederate Monument?"

Following her lead, I would reply, "Yes, Mom. I asked for a whole day off."

Appreciating the ways I have so often anticipated her needs, she would say, "You know, they don't really give any food here. There is a shortage of food." And in the car, on our way to the restaurant, she would inquire about her mother—how she was doing, whether she was healthy. She resurrected her mother, who had been dead for fifty-five years. My mother was both there and here at the same time. Is this forgetting? Is this remembering? It is that third space not defined by either side of the binary, that suspended space between a failed remembering and an incomplete forgetting. In this space, against the normativitizing force of predetermined rules, she dared to mix and piece together the fragmented souvenirs, not to their previous wholeness, but to the wholeness-in-the-making.[27] My mother inhabited this third space between remembering and forgetting. This is an in-between space called "home."

~

My mother was called back to her eternal home on March 14, 2017. That day a nor'easter had swept across New York and Pennsylvania, bringing over one foot of snow, erasing the world in white. We were not there when she decided to go peacefully. But the day before, my sisters and I anointed her feet with perfumed sandalwood oil, just as Mary anoints Jesus's feet (John 12:1–8). We sat on her bed each jealously vying for her now failing attention and argued about who her favorite daughter was. We were laughing and teasing then; we did not expect her to go so fast with the falling snow.

As I contemplate my journey of caring, mourning, and grieving, I too am found in that middle, in-between space. It is the space between death and resurrection—the space between Good Friday and Easter Sunday. I was in that Holy Saturday space of remaining and waiting, the space of complicated and ambiguous grief. Remaining in that abyss, not alone but accompanied by the Holy Spirit, in retrospect was my spiritual journey.

The Spirit remains with us in that abyss, that middle space between death and life, where, as Shelley Rambo declares, the divine breath meets the human breath, where "the silent human cry meets the silent divine cry."[28]

27. Trinh, *When the Moon Waxes Red*, 157.
28. Rambo, *Spirit and Trauma*, 170.

Part II: Grieving

Because, the Spirit is love. And in that abyss, life must be witnessed because life cannot be seen.[29] Witnessing is a way of enfleshing the ghost. With love's conviction, it is testifying and being present to the life that remains.

The abyss calls us. It calls us to witness. In the middle, life cannot be seen, *life must be witnessed*. By this, I do not ask to be delivered *from* the abyss. Rather, my journey of care and love and the attendant grace that enveloped me was a way of being *in* the abyss.[30] It was a dutiful practice of witnessing life arising from the fragments, ordered and re-ordered.[31] That is where I found myself.

In the end, I have come to realize that my mother's story, our story, "is neither a tragic one nor a triumphant one but, in fact, a story of divine remaining, the story of love that survives."[32] My witness, like a souvenir, however fragmented it may be, calls to mind my mother's life, un/seen but present and alive.

QUESTIONS FOR REFLECTION

1. Currently we are in a period of multiple pandemics—COVID-19, anti-Black violence, anti-Asian violence, and economic and ecological crisis. What does "being called into the abyss" mean for you, and what are you being asked to witness?

2. During the COVID-19 crisis, many who lost their loved ones were not able to see, touch, and be present with them as they were dying. How might the concept of "ambiguous loss" help to voice the experience of incompleteness and lack of closure?

3. What are the stories and memories of your mother's life that were written, erased, and written over to create her living human document? What are yours?

---

29. Rambo, *Spirit and Trauma*, 137.
30. Rambo, *Spirit and Trauma*, 172.
31. Rambo, *Spirit and Trauma*, 172.
32. Rambo, *Spirit and Trauma*, 172.

7

Satisfy Us with Your Goodness
Caring and Grieving for My Mother, Tova

MYCHAL B. SPRINGER

THE AMAZING THING ABOUT being a spiritual caregiver, and a pastoral educator in particular, is that the personal is the professional, meaning that I am both living my life and studying my life at the same time. Anton Boisen coined the term "living human document" to talk about the centrality that people need to have in teaching us religious truths, and I am in this tradition as I think about the place that my relationship with my mother has had in orienting me spiritually.[1]

In February 2017, corresponding with the Hebrew month of Shevat, I received a call from my mother's hospice nurse as I sat with my hospice clinical pastoral education (CPE) interns and taught them about spiritual care for people with dementia, drawing on my experience with my mom and her dementia as my great teacher. It became clear to me that my mother had shifted into a new stage of dying, so I told my group that I now needed to go and be with my mom. I didn't return to work until two weeks later, after I had buried my mom and sat shiva (the traditional week of mourning).

---

1. Asquith, *Vision from a Little Known Country*.

Part II: Grieving

My decision to step away from my regular life at that moment in order to devote myself to caring for my mom had a tremendous impact on my grieving. For the years of my mother's declining health and the months of her being in hospice I regularly checked in with myself to make sure that I was feeling good enough about the balance in my life. I felt guilt at times for not doing enough for my mom, and guilt about not showing up enough for the rest of my family (but not guilt about not doing enough work), but I also felt at an overall level of comfort with my decisions in the face of the physical, emotional, and financial realities of our lives. And I was guided by an awareness that my mother's physical life was limited, treasuring sacred moments with her even as I also felt pain and helplessness. I think a lot about that moment when I put aside the rest of my life and stepped into caring for my mother as my sole focus for the last week of her life. That week was all love. While I had been preparing for my mother's death for a long time,* and we had finished any unfinished business a long time ago, that week allowed for a final cementing of my mom and me in an unbreakable bond.

---

preparing for my mother's death for a long time

Journeying with a loved one who has a chronic illness gives us the opportunity to prepare ourselves for their deaths ... at least, in some ways. Such preparation is not linear, and not characterized by things we can check off on a to-do list. Reading Mychal's journey of preparing for her mother's death highlighted clear distinctions for me in how I prepared for each of my parents' deaths twenty-four years apart.

Because my dad was only sixty-three years old, and because he had been the paragon of strength in our family, we believed God was invested in healing this man who did so much to help others. I was not emotionally able to prepare for the possibility of Dad dying.

When Dad was dying and Mom was grieving him, I felt like a trapeze artist flying high in an unfamiliar world without a net. While I did believe God was my ultimate net, I also believed that God was the decider of whether my dad would live or die. So, how I approached God during that period was often complex. At that time, the thought of "preparing" for Dad's death was tantamount to a faithless acceptance of his death as inevitable. Such an acceptance I regarded as a betrayal to my dad. At times, I feared that any preparation or acceptance of his dying on my part would speed up his death. As a consequence, I had very little preparation for his death.

> Two-plus decades later when Mom was dying, I was much more able to prepare for her death. Although Mom's dementia made it progressively more difficult to have the kinds of conversations I would have liked, losing her cognitively facilitated my preparations for losing her physically. It prepared me to live without her. It trained me to connect with her spiritually, which is how I have connected with her since her physical death. —Cari

Eight months before my mother died, my mother couldn't breathe and her aide called 911, which her agency's policy required. Though I knew that my mother did not want to go to the hospital under any circumstances, and though she had her Do Not Resuscitate (DNR) orders taped up throughout her apartment, it was only then that I learned that the DNR did not cover respiratory distress, as the paramedic told me over the phone, hanging up on me so that he could rush my mother to the hospital. I met my mother as she was taken out of the ambulance, escorted her into the emergency room, and told the doctor that her wish was to go home. He told me that my mother would die within forty-eight hours. As her health care proxy I was in a position to make that decision, but the doctor actually helped me when he requested that I speak with my siblings to make sure we were all on the same page. After tearful conversation, we were. So my mother and I spent a quiet day in a private room in the emergency department while the social worker arranged for home hospice intake. I sang to her and witnessed her peaceful resting. As a hospital chaplain I had been in this peaceful place many times before. And in my own life, with my brother-in-law, who died much too young, and with my father, I'd also had the honor of being in that sacred space, escorting into death. It was Shabbat, my father's *yahrzeit* (the fourth anniversary of his death), and I knew that my mother would embrace it as a good day to die. She had always done everything with my father in life, and this would be a way to do even her dying tied to him.*
When the hospice intake and transportation were arranged, I escorted my mother home. On the way out of the emergency department, I asked the nurse to take my mother's blood pressure one last time, but then I changed my mind, figuring that it didn't matter at that point. And we left.

---

even her dying tied to him

"As Daddy always says . . ." These were the words Mom spoke for many years after Dad died. She echoed certain common phrases of his as if he were still speaking these words. Inside her heart

> and mind he continued to speak clearly. The intimacy of the connection my mom and dad shared made it possible for her to hear him well even across the years and decades. Mom's continued intimate connection with Dad helped my brothers and me believe in and cultivate our own connections with Dad after his death.
>
> It is often said that intimacy can best be described as "into me see." Seeing clearly into the hearts and listening deeply into the souls of others enables a capacity of emotional and spiritual connection that transcends death. Mom showed me that again and again. And now, I am experiencing that with her. —Cari

When we got back to my mother's apartment, we put her in to bed. I crawled in next to her, exhausted. The aide brought me some food, knowing that I had not eaten all day. As I sat next to my mother, she turned to me and seemed to perk up a bit. I asked her if she was hungry and she said yes. So we took her out of bed, brought her to the table, and gave her some dinner. By the time the hospice intake nurse visited my mom a couple of hours later my mother failed the intake assessment because the hospice team assessed her as has having had an acute episode, which is to say that the hospice said they did not consider her to be dying.[2]

I was devastated. Having spent the day actively preparing for her death, it was painful to me to be told that she was not dying in the next day or so, to have to pull back into the nebulous world of slow dying. I knew that my mother belonged in hospice, that I would have to say goodbye to her all over again, just not knowing when that would be. I was afraid of what the days and weeks ahead would look like, how much more she would suffer, how much sicker and more dependent she would become. I knew that she would have wanted to be released from life that day and that I had failed her by not knowing that I needed a MOLST (Medical Orders about Life Sustaining Treatment) form that could have protected her from the ambulance and the treatment she received on the way to the hospital—treatment that had tipped her back into life.

As I sorted through my grief, my helplessness, my disappointment, and my fear I found myself returning again and again to the liturgical poem *Adon Olam*. It proclaims:

> I place my spirit in God's care; my body too can feel God near.
> When I sleep, as when I wake, God is with me, I have no fear.[3]

---

2. In order for a person to be eligible for hospice, a doctor needs to give the person a prognosis of having six months or less to live.

3. *Siddur Lev Shalem*, 211.

The Hebrew begins, "Into Your hand I entrust my spirit." (Ps 31:6 NJPS) The translation I used moved away from the anthropomorphic, but I love the image of God's spiritual hands. I turned to those hands in that experience of being undone. I would say these words with my hands turned up, feeling God's hands holding up my mom, and holding me up as I held her up. I leaned on the embodied sense of being held up to help me lean into trusting that she and I would continue to be held up in the time ahead, no matter what would unfold. I was afraid of what the caregiving would need to look like to help her feel fully cared for. Would I fail her again?

The word "my body" in this line is a translation of the Hebrew word *g'viyati*, which means "my body" and "my corpse"—a living body and a dead body. The literal translation is, "and with my spirit, my corpse." There's a promise that just as God holds us in life, God holds us in death. I knew that my mother was not afraid to die, that she welcomed her timely death, that she trusted that she would be reunited with my father and that it would be good. We had spoken of this regularly. But in this incremental process of dying, I was living with "ambiguous loss," the process of losing in living, the intertwining of having and not having, of being both a live and a dead body.[4] That day I saw my mother as the dying person she was, and then I needed to welcome her back into the world of the living, knowing that her sojourn with us would be very limited. Entrusting her to God's hands meant giving up any sense that I could protect her from the slow decline that lay ahead, even as I was determined to protect her from any more trips to the hospital.

Later that week my mother *was* admitted into home hospice, thanks to the intervention of her doctor, who agreed that she was in fact at the end of her life. I spread the word about the importance of advanced care planning and the existence of the MOLST form.[5] Many people benefitted from my experience with my mom. It helped me turn my distress into necessary wisdom.

The attentive care and love of the hospice team enabled my mother to live for eight more months. Many people don't know that hospice can extend someone's life, as the team pays close attention to the intimate details of a person's needs and adjusts accordingly. As my mother stabilized, I found pleasure in moments of connection with her. She was not suffering. Her extended life was not a burden to her. It was okay that she was still

---

4. Boss, *Ambiguous Loss*.
5. See https://molst.org/.

alive. I would never have felt this way without hospice. On the day of her admission I called in the chaplain—a former student and dear colleague of mine—and he lovingly visited my mom every week, bringing her challah and helping her bring in Shabbat. And I also asked for the music therapist. Meredith was an incredible blessing in my mother's life. Together we worked out a playlist for her to sing with my mom—Hebrew songs from my mother's childhood that Meredith had in her repertoire in transliteration. The effort she made to embrace my mother in her own language moved me. Meredith told me that she often saved visiting my mom for the end of the day because she felt deeply cared for by my mom, who would always thank her for coming, saying, "I love you." I loved my mother's love for Meredith and everyone who cared for her, a testament to my mom's embracing the care that she needed, walking deeply in gratitude.

About thirty-six hours before she died, my mother sang happy birthday to my husband, Jonathan. My mother loved singing happy birthday. At Thanksgiving a few months after my father died, we had sung happy birthday to my mom, who was turning eighty-two. When we were done, she asked us to sing happy birthday to my dad, since their birthdays were only three days apart. As she was dying, when we told her it was Jonathan's birthday, she joined in the singing. These were the last words she spoke. Sitting in a circle around her bed singing with her were my brother and sister, my daughters, Jonathan, my aunt and uncle (my mother's brother), who had just arrived from Israel, and me. That circle contained a whole world, and we could all feel that she, like Abraham, had reached the moment of being *zaken v'save'a*, "old and contented" (Gen 25:8 NJPS). She brought me into this world, and I helped ease her into the next world.*

I helped ease her into the next world

Like Mychal, I was able to be fully present in the last week of my mom's life, and it deeply affected my grieving. While I did not believe she was dying until the last three days, it became clear when the hospice team described all the phases that Mom would pass through on her way to death, with instructions on how and when to administer her morphine. It was as if a calm set into my body to help support her needs in methodical and compassionate ways.

I cannot imagine the pain and suffering that is amplified in these COVID-19 times when a beloved family member is enduring this passage from life to death alone. My heart aches to hear that a mother who ushered her child or children into life cannot be surrounded and touched by them in the moment of her parting. —Linda

I know that not everyone is blessed with a final week, or whatever the equivalent might look like. That many mothers die too soon or too suddenly or too messily.* And with the apex of the COVID-19 pandemic just behind us in New York—and numbers rising around the country and around the world—I have a new appreciation for the pain of all the people who died in hospital rooms away from the people they loved the most, and for those who loved them but who were not able to take up their posts at bedside. This experience has only reinforced my belief that the kind of care that we are able to offer our mothers in their dying effects our grief.

That many mothers die too soon or too suddenly or too messily

Joan Didion wrote these words as she grieved over the loss of her husband, John Gregory Dunne, from a sudden massive heart attack. —Kathy

Life changes in the instant. The ordinary instant. At some point, in the interest of remembering what seemed most striking about what had happened, I considered adding those words, "the ordinary instant." I saw immediately that there would be no need to add the word, "ordinary," because there would be no forgetting it: the word never left my mind. It was in fact the ordinary nature of everything preceding the event that prevented me from truly believing it had happened, absorbing it, incorporating it, getting past it. I recognize now that there was nothing unusual in this: confronted with sudden disaster we all focus on how unremarkable the circumstances were in which the unthinkable occurred.[6]

My brother, Jonathan, and I stayed with my mother in a vigil on the last night of her life, giving her morphine as she needed it—an intimate dance of reading her body as she did the work of transitioning, keeping pace with her the best we could: not too much medicine, not too little. She died in the early morning.* After she died, we waited with her until the funeral home came to take her body, and then we escorted her down the hall. As we walked behind her, I turned to my brother and said, "She stopped

---

6. Didion, *The Year of Magical Thinking*, 3–4.

breathing, right?" The line between life and death feeling so permeable, the reality of her death still so hard to absorb.

She died in the early morning

Mychal's story brought back memories of the day my mother died.

My mother was hospitalized with pneumonia for the second time in three months. When I arrived at the hospital, I found her alone in a room, in respiratory distress, lungs filling with fluid, struggling to breathe. I screamed for the nurses, identified myself as her daughter and the health care proxy. I told them my mother was ninety-three years old, in late stage dementia, and all I wanted was for her not to suffer. After administering medication to drain fluid, the nurses went to check her chart. They returned later saying they could not locate her chart and couldn't confirm the proxy!!

I demanded to see a doctor. In this tiny local hospital, there was only one doctor in the building, and he was serving as the ER physician. They refused to call him away from the ER. I got fierce. "You are telling me *you* cannot locate my mother's chart and you will not *allow me* to see the doctor?!?"

Within minutes, he was on the floor.

A gentle, alert young doctor, moonlighting from a first-rate Manhattan hospital, assessed the situation quickly, placed an order, and apologized. He put his arm around me as I told him stories about what a devoted mother she had been. When he left, I stayed by her side, on her bed, until she died.

My husband and I drove back to Philadelphia in the wee hours of the morning. After two hours of sleep, I rose and dressed. It was the day of my younger daughter's high school graduation.

In the auditorium with my husband, my older daughter, my best friend, and her daughter, at whose wedding we'd be dancing within days, we stood arm in arm, weeping tears of grief-joy-awe at the power of love and at how the curve of the generations can intersect itself, forming nodes and portals through which we glimpse the secret architecture of our lives. —Bobbi

And then we needed to say goodbye to her amazing caregivers. Their care and love for my mother had sustained her throughout the end of her life, and our gratitude was beyond anything we could express. We wept with them and grieved together. As religious Christians, Joyce and Irene were curious about the Jewish rituals that would follow. They were disappointed that there would be no wake. As their disappointment registered on me,

I realized that they were looking for one more intimate moment of being with my mother now that she was at peace. So I told them about *shmira*, the Jewish custom of sitting with the dead body and performing a spiritual guardianship as she transitions to the next world, and invited them to join me. The three of us sat with my mom in the funeral home, reciting psalms. I had never imagined that we would be my mother's *shmira* trio—Joyce, a Seventh-day Adventist from Jamaica; Irene, a Catholic Puerto Rican; and me, a rabbi. But our presence alongside my mother's body felt like a tremendously holy way of honoring the life she lived and the way that her life opened up into new relationships, even at the end of her life.

The week of caring flowed into the week of grieving. My mother remained at the center. Where her body had been at the center during the week of her dying, her life became the center during the first week of my grieving. Many people have written beautifully about shiva. I experienced it as an unparalleled gift.* Again, in the midst of COVID-19-based lockdown, I am intensely aware of what a blessing it is to be able to gather in person for shiva, and of the ways that social distancing have challenged and changed the grieving process. I am thankful that my mother died in a time before COVID-19. During shiva for my mom I sat with family and was comforted.* People from my life came to my home and listened to our stories, witnessed our tears, enabled us to pray in community, helped us to say mourners' kaddish, and brought food.

---

an unparalleled gift

Through this piece, I could feel Mychal's deep connection to her spiritual tradition and how the ritual forms of Judaism held her through her mourning process, allowing her to rest in loving connection in the midst of profound loss.

I belonged to what is termed an "underritualized"[7] family. We did not engage in any formal rituals to mark significant life changes in our home or participate in larger social rituals. So, when my mother died, there were no symbolic actions available that could "hold me up when I couldn't walk" (as Kathy expressed during our conversations) and provide a way to feel into the cavernous reality of living without a mother for the rest of my life.

As I write this, I now see how significant this early experience with failed ritualized space has been in forming my life

---

7. Roberts, "Setting the Frame."

choices. For over two decades I have centered my life on building and supporting a Zen Buddhist community, devoting myself to a highly ritualized and deeply communal religious practice. As a psychotherapist, I am equally devoted to creating a ritualized space for bringing forward pain hiding underneath the surface of things. In Zen, we talk about our spiritual activities as practices. We practice ritual so that it is available for ourselves, for our community, and for future generations, and in honor of those who have passed it on to us. We keep it alive so that its medicine is available when needed. In speaking with my sisters in mourning, I came to further appreciate all those who keep mourning ritual practices available for their communities. As Mychal noted in one of our conversations, it is "a life commitment to live inside of ritual, knowing that it only exists because we create it."—Laura

---

I sat with family and was comforted

The Jewish tradition of shiva is similar to the traditions of diverse communities within Latino culture. For us, the time for grieving varies from family to family; it can range from one week to a full year. One of the ways that we were able to begin our grief process was to keep Mom's body in her home for twenty-four hours after she died. I was surprised when the hospice team let us know that we could choose when to arrange for the mortuary to pick up her body. I had always thought the deceased needed to be taken away as soon as possible. Our whole family deeply appreciated the opportunity to say their goodbyes while Mom was in the safe space that she called home. Even the children, no matter what age, were very comfortable hugging her lifeless body, kissing her, and speaking to her with the full belief that she was still with us. That experience made a profound impact on how each of us was able to feel so connected to Mom's spirit. —Linda

The surprise for me was that in the moment that my mother died I felt that I knew her completely. But as I sat shiva, and people asked questions about my mother and her life, I realized that she was in so many ways a mystery to me. Shiva awakened in me a desire to know more, to ask her questions that I had never thought to ask. To ask her questions that I had asked many times but that she had never managed to answer. Having my uncle at shiva gave me access to his understanding of my mom, his beautiful rendering of his older sister—who joined the *Haganah* at sixteen and fought for the creation of the State of Israel (as a secretary), who learned to swallow paper, in case classified documents were in danger of being compromised. And suddenly I couldn't believe that she had slipped through my fingers and now it was too late. It broke my heart that all I had were fragments. But every day of shiva opened up a whole new world. The fragments shifted and my relationship to them shifted. The grief was alive, an organism.

Every day as people piled into my apartment to help us make a *minyan* (the required prayer quorum), I would serve as *shelichat tzibur*, the prayer leader. This is the special mitzvah for the mourner. With the voices of the minyan behind me I would be held as I chanted the traditional liturgy. And different phrases from the liturgy would announce themselves in new ways, catching my attention and letting me know that they were included in the liturgy from the beginning just for that moment. One of these was the prayer known as *Avot*, the ancestors, the first blessing in the Amidah, the prayer at the center of every prayer service.

Blessed are you, our God and the God of our Ancestors . . . The prayer is rooted in the idea of *zechut avot*, the merit of our ancestors. Our relationship with God is secure and abiding, no matter what we do, because of the merit of our ancestors, who lived in ways that engendered such a strong bond with the divine that the abundance of their merit has spilled over throughout the generations, and continues to wash over us, even now. And now my mother was an ancestor. As I recited this prayer every day, three times a day, in community, I felt my mother transitioning into her ancestorhood, securing her place in my life in a new way. She was gone and not gone. My journey with my dead mother was beginning.

The second prayer in the Amidah is *mehayeh ha'metim*, who gives life to the dead.[8] As a rabbinical student I had been greatly disturbed by the challenge of embracing a belief in life after death. It was the process of being with people as they died that loosened my attachment to rationalism and allowed me to embrace the living that continues after death. As a new mourner I proclaimed my belief in the possibilities of life after death and opened myself to discovering what this would look like for me and my mom.

On the Shabbat that fell during shiva I went to shul (synagogue) and recited the special blessing for Shabbat found in the Amidah. This was my mother's favorite prayer in her final years of life. In fact, it became her favorite song. If I asked her what song she wanted to sing, this would be the song she would ask me to sing, over and over again, and so I did. As

---

8. *Siddur Lev Shalem*, 160.

Part II: Grieving

I recited the blessing that Shabbat, I knew that I would always find my mother in the recitation of those words. As I meditated on the words, I discovered something that had always been there—that the words themselves had a particular connection to my mother. The phrase that leapt out at me was *sabeinu mi'tuvekha*, "satisfy us with your goodness."[9] My mother had always lived out a simple spirituality of gratitude, conveying a deep satisfaction with the smallest of gifts. As a child I had always wanted my mother to want more for herself, disappointed that she was not more ambitious, didn't strive more. She was a stay-at-home mom until my brother and sister and I were able to be at home on our own, which was when she started running my father's oral surgery practice. She was humble. And she hid her embarrassment about never having finished high school, only disclosing this to me when I was in my twenties, when she sought my blessing as she wrestled with abandoning her long-standing hope to complete her GED, realizing that it was too much for her. I readily gave my blessing and felt a deep sadness that she had felt the need to hide.

Hiding had been more of a theme in my mother's life than I had known growing up, though I was aware of how hard it was for her to share with me her memories of growing up. I didn't realize that trauma had prevented those memories from forming. That all she had was fragments. It was while I was in rabbinical school, interviewing her as part of an assignment for my first pastoral care class, that she disclosed that her parents had placed her in an orphanage when she was three years old. Being born and raised in British Mandate Palestine, there was little food for my mother to eat, and my grandparents could not both work and take care of her, so the orphanage was the only option. As I absorbed the tremendous pain of this disclosure, my mother reassured me that it was okay, that her parents visited her each week. While her acceptance took me aback in the moment, I came to understand that she lived with a deep faith in God's goodness and was satisfied, *sabeinu mi'tuvekha*. And as I examined this phrase more carefully after her death, I received a sign from my mother. The word *tuvekha* is shaped by the three-letter root: *t-o-v* (actually two letters, but who's counting?) The word *tov* means "good." And my mother's name was Tova, the good one, translated from the Yiddish Gitel, who was her grandmother, who lived and died in Poland. So here was my mother all along, and I was only now finding her. I derived great comfort in knowing that this phrase

---

9. *Siddur Lev Shalem*, 163.

would be engraved on my mother's tombstone, a testament to how she lived and a legacy she left behind, a portal into ongoing relationship.

Among the many amazing people who supported me during shiva and in the weeks and months that followed, throughout the year of mourning that is observed for a parent, there were many people who were current and past students of mine. Since aging and dying and grieving is at the heart of my professional life, I had a strong sense that my life and my grief was the text. I could see how much some of my students wanted to comfort me, and how relieved they were to discover that their presence was in fact a comfort to me. Coming out of a transformative experience of caring for my mother, I understood with great clarity that I had an obligation to allow others to care for me. And I needed it. I was aware that this caring allowed me to move into being an orphan with a sense that there was still love in this world for me.

Not long ago one of my CPE students was pregnant with her first child. She discovered that many of her patients were seeing their mothers or calling for their mothers at the end of their lives. She and I would explore what it meant to her that mothers had a special place for so many people as they approached death; that their mothers hovered as they prepared to transition to the next world. For her this was a challenging observation, as she grappled with her estranged relationship with her own mother on the eve of becoming a mother herself. For me, this always evoked my mother and her birthday-deathbed scene. The intertwined beginnings and endings. I felt my mother's availability to me as I walked with my student. My grief for my mother, and my ongoing relationship with her, helped me to escort my student as she escorted the dying people in her care reaching for their mothers at the end, while she lived with the unavailability of her own mother. There was a repaired wholeness for me in all the mothers intersecting. And then, when my student gave birth and became a mother, my mother-self joined her in a tremendous exaltation. The nearness of my mother, despite her death, infused my rejoicing in the miracle of birth—the birth of the baby and the birth of the mother. The preciousness of it all was overwhelming.

Paradoxically, moving towards caring and dying can be a profound way of moving toward life. And the grieving in the aftermath of a loss is both a pulling away from the rhythms of a bustling life and a process of becoming equipped to reenter life with a fuller sense of the preciousness of the gift of life and the opportunities to live fully. My mother would often

Part II: Grieving

quote the saying: "Who is wise, the one who learns from everyone."[10] When we value each and every human being as holding some essential wisdom, then we ourselves are being wise. By valuing the wisdom of each person, even those of us who are in need of endless care, we gain a deep understanding of how to navigate our days on earth.

QUESTIONS FOR REFLECTION

1. Can you describe a time when you received a memory of your mother, after her death that filled in a missing piece that you didn't even know you were waiting for?
2. What has helped you to recognize when you are called to leave the routine of your life and make yourself available to care for another?
3. What more might you need to do to engage in advanced care planning with the ones you love so that you and each of your loved ones will be able to serve effectively as a health care proxy?

---

10. Pirkei Avot 4:1 (my translation).

Resources

Anzaldúa, Gloria. *Borderlands/La Frontera: The New Mestiza.* San Francisco: Spinsters/Aunt Lute, 1987.

Asquith, Glenn H. Jr., ed. *Vision from a Little Known Country: A Boisen Reader.* Decatur, GA: Journal of Pastoral Care Publications, 1992.

Benson, Tracey. "The Museum of the Personal: Souvenirs and Nostalgia." MA thesis, Queensland University of Technology, 2001.

Bhabha, Homi K. *The Location of Culture.* London: Routledge, 1994.

Bieler, Yaakov, "Parshat Ki Tissa: Broken Tablets – Embarrassment or Inspiration?" *Text & Texture*, February 11, 2011. http://text.rcarabbis.org/parshat-ki-tissa-broken-tablets-embarrassment-or-inspiration-by-yaakov-bieler/

Bonanno, George A. *The Other Side of Sadness: What the New Science of Bereavement Tells Us about Life after Loss.* New York: Basic Books, 2010.

Boss, Pauline. *Ambiguous Loss: Learning to Live with Unresolved Grief.* Cambridge: Harvard University Press, 1999.

Brener, Anne. *Mourning & Mitzvah: A Guided Journal for Walking the Mourner's Path through Grief and Healing.* 2nd ed. Woodstock, VT: Jewish Lights, 2001.

Cho, Grace M. *Haunting the Korean Diaspora: Shame, Secrecy, and the Forgotten War.* Minneapolis: University of Minnesota Press, 2008.

The Conversation Project. https://www.theconversationproject.org/.

Cowan, Rachel, and Linda Thal. *Wise Aging.* Springfield, NJ: Behrman House, 2015.

Didion, Joan. *The Year of Magical Thinking.* New York: Knopf, 2005.

Doka, Kenneth J., and Amy S. Tucci, eds. *The Longest Loss: Alzheimer's Disease and Dementia.* Washington, DC: Hospice Foundation of America, 2015.

Edelman, Hope. *Motherless Daughters: The Legacy of Loss.* New York: Dell, 1994.

Ellison, Koshin Paley, and Matt Weingast, eds. *Awake at the Bedside: Contemplative Teachings on Palliative and End-of-Life Care.* Somerville, MA: Wisdom, 2016.

Elwell, Sue Levi, and Nancy Kreimer, eds. *Chapters of the Heart: Jewish Women Sharing the Torah of Our Lives.* Eugene, OR: Cascade Books, 2013.

Fishel, Deirdre, dir. *Care: The Hidden World of Elder Care.* Produced by Mind's Eye Productions. New York: New Day Films, 2017. https://www.newday.com/film/care/.

Friedman, Dayle. "Seeking the *Tzelem*: Making Sense of Dementia." *Reconstructionist* 70/2 (2006) 43–55.

Fromm, M. Gerald. *Lost in Transmission: Studies in Trauma across Generations.* London: Karnac, 2012.

Resources

Gardner, Aidan. "'I Put My Own Life on Hold': The Pain and Joy of Caring for Parents." *New York Times*, September 5, 2019. https://www.nytimes.com/2019/09/05/reader-center/taking-care-of-elderly-relatives.html/.

Gawande, Atul. *Being Mortal: Medicine and What Matters in the End*. New York: Metropolitan, 2014.

Gordon, Avery. *Ghostly Matters: Haunting and the Sociological Imagination*. Minneapolis: University of Minnesota Press, 2008.

Gordon, Mary. *Circling My Mother: A Memoir*. New York: Pantheon, 2007.

Greenspan, Miriam. *Healing through the Dark Emotions: The Wisdom of Grief, Fear, and Despair*. Boston: Shambhala, 2003.

Groome, Thomas H. *What Makes Us Catholic: Eight Gifts for Life*. San Francisco: HarperSanFrancisco, 2002.

Guerrette, Marie-France, dir. *Unmothered*. Montreal: National Film Board of Canada, 2019. https://www.nfb.ca/film/unmothered/.

Halifax, Joan. *Being with Dying: Cultivating Compassion and Fearlessness in the Presence of Death*. Boston: Shambhala, 2008.

Hodgman, George. *Bettyville: A Memoir*. New York: Penguin, 2015.

Hong, Jong-chan, dir. *Dear My Friends*. Written by Noh Hee-kyung. Starring Go Hyun-jung et al. 16 episodes aired from May 13, 2016, to July 2, 2016, on tvN, and KST, South Korea.

"How to Complete a MOLST." MOLST: Medical Orders for Life-Sustaining Treatment. https://molst.org/how-to-complete-a-molst/.

Jung, Da-min. "Separated Families Cry Out for Humanitarian Policy for Reunion." Interview with Joy Lee Bokshin Gebhard. *Korea Times*, October 6, 2019. Updated October 8, 2019. http://www.koreatimes.co.kr/www/news/nation/2019/10/103_276668.html/.

Kalanithi, Paul. *When Breath Becomes Air*. New York: Random House, 2016.

Krauss, Dan, dir. *Extremis*. Starring Monica Bhargava and Jessica Zitter. Produced by f/8 Filmworks. Distributed by Netflix, 2016.

Kumar, Sameet. *Grieving Mindfully*. Oakland, CA: New Harbinger, 2005.

Laverone, Kenneth J., Jr. "Is There a Place for Curanderismo in Pastoral Care to People of Mexican Descent?" MA thesis, Graduate Theological Union, 1994.

Lee, Chang-rae. "Coming Home Again." *New Yorker*, October 16, 1995. https://www.newyorker.com/magazine/1995/10/16/coming-home-again

Levine, Stephen. *Unattended Sorrow: Recovering from Loss and Reviving the Heart*. Emmaus, PA: Rodale, 2005.

Levine, Stephen, and Ondrea Levine. *Who Dies? An Investigation of Conscious Living and Conscious Dying*. New York: Random House, 1982.

Mace, Nancy L., and Peter V. Rabins. *The 36-Hour Day: A Family Guide to Caring for People Who Have Alzheimer's Disease, Other Dementias, and Memory Loss*, 6th ed. A Johns Hopkins Press Health Book. Baltimore: Johns Hopkins University Press, 2017.

Marlene Meyerson JCC Manhattan. "What Matters" (web page). Marlene Meyerson JCC Manhattan. https://mmjccm.org/what-matters/.

McPhee, Larkin, writer and director. *Caring for Mom & Dad*. Starring Meryl Streep. DVD. Arlington, VA: PBS, 2015. https://www.pbs.org/show/caring-mom-dad/.

Menakem, Resmaa. *My Grandmother's Hands: Racialized Trauma and the Pathway to Mending Our Hearts and Bodies*. Las Vegas: Central Recovery, 2017.

Metz, Johannes Baptist. *Faith in History and Society*. Translated by David Smith. New York: Seabury, 1980.

Resources

Moore, Thomas. *Care of the Soul.* 25th anniversary ed. New York: HarperPerennial, 2016.

Morton, Nelle. *The Journey Is Home.* Boston: Beacon, 1985.

Moses, Sarah M. *Ethics and the Elderly: The Challenge of Long-Term Care.* Maryknoll, NY: Orbis, 2015.

Nhat Hanh, Thich. *No Death, No Fear: Comforting Wisdom for Life.* New York: Riverhead, 2002.

Nouwen, Henri J. M. *A Spirituality of Caregiving.* The Henri Nouwen Spirituality Series. Nashville: Upper Room, 2011.

Oliver, Mary. *Thirst: Poems.* Boston: Beacon, 2006.

Olson, Tillie, ed. *Mother to Daughter, Daughter to Mother.* Old Westbury, NY: Feminist Press, 1984.

Ostaseski, Frank. *The Five Invitations: Discovering What Death Can Teach Us about Living Fully.* New York: Flatiron, 2017

Owens, Virginia Stem. *Caring for Mother: A Daughter's Long Goodbye.* Louisville: Westminster John Knox, 2007.

Palmer, Parker. *On the Brink of Everything: Grace, Gravity, and Getting Old.* Oakland, CA: Berrett-Koehler, 2018.

Pak, Su Yon. "Contemplating Radical Love." *Inheritance,* 64, July 19, 2019. https://www.inheritancemag.com/issues/64-milestones

Poo, Ai-Jen, *The Age of Dignity: Preparing for the Elder Boom in a Changing America.* New York: New Press, 2015.

Porter, Edwardo. "Why Aren't More Women Working? They're Caring for Parents." *New York Times,* August 29, 2019. https://www.nytimes.com/2019/08/29/business/economy/labor-family-care.html/.

Potts, Daniel C., et al., eds. *Seasons of Caring: Meditations for Alzheimer's and Dementia Caregivers.* Washington DC: ClergyAgainstAlzheimer's Network, 2014.

Prechtel, Martin. *The Smell of Rain on Dust: Grief and Praise.* Berkeley, CA: North Atlantic, 2015.

Rambo, Shelley. *Spirit and Trauma: A Theology of Remaining.* Louisville: Westminster John Knox, 2010.

ReImagine: End of Life. https://letsreimagine.org/.

Remen, Rachel Naomi. *Kitchen Table Wisdom: Stories That Heal.* 10th anniversary ed. New York: Berkeley, 2006.

Riemer, Jack, ed. *Wrestling with the Angel: Jewish Insights on Death and Mourning.* New York: Schocken, 1995.

Roberts, Janine. "Setting the Frame: Definition, Functions, and Typology of Rituals." In *Rituals in Families & Family Therapy,* edited by Evan Imber-Black et al., 3–48. New York: Norton, 1988.

Rukeyser, Muriel. "Käthe Kollwitz." In *The Collected Poems of Muriel Rukeyser,* edited by Janet E. Kaufman and Anne F. Herzog, with Jan Heller Levi, 460–64. Pittsburgh: University of Pittsburgh Press, 2006.

Saha, Somnath, et al. "Patient Centeredness, Cultural Competence and Healthcare Quality." *Journal of the National Medical Association* 100/11 (2008) 1275–85.

Siddur Lev Shalem: For Shabbat & Festivals. New York: The Rabbinical Assembly, 2016.

Singh, Kathleen Dowling. *The Grace in Aging: Awaken as You Grow Older.* Somerville, MA: Wisdom, 2014.

Swinton, John. *Becoming Friends of Time: Disability, Timefullness, and Gentle Discipleship.* Studies in Religion, Theology, and Disability. Waco: Baylor University Press, 2016.

Resources

———. *Dementia: Living in the Memories of God*. Grand Rapids: Eerdmans, 2012.

Taussig, Hal, ed. *A New New Testament: A Bible for the Twenty-First Century Combining Traditional and Newly Discovered Texts*. Boston: Houghton Mifflin Harcourt, 2013.

Taussig, Hal, et al. *The Thunder: Perfect Mind, A New Translation and Introduction*. New York: Palgrave Macmillan, 2010.

Tirabbasi, Maren C., et al. *Caring for Ourselves While Caring for Our Elders*. Cleveland: Pilgrim, 2007.

Trinh, T. Minh-ha. *Elsewhere, Within Here: Immigration, Refugeeism, and the Boundary Event*. New York: Routledge, 2011.

———. "Far Away, From Home: The Comma Between." In *Elsewhere, Within Here: Immigration, Refugeeism, and the Boundary Event*, 11–25. New York: Routledge, 2011.

———. *When the Moon Waxes Red: Representation, Gender and Cultural Politics*. New York: Routledge, 1991.

Unser, Don J. *Chasing Dichos through Chimayó*. Querencias Series. Albuquerque: University of New Mexico Press, 2014.

Vallgårda, Karen. "Keeping Secrets." *Aeon*, November 6, 2019. https://aeon.co/essays/why-family-secrets-should-sometimes-stay-under-lock-and-key/.

Van Der Kolk, Bessel. *The Body Keeps the Score: Brain, Mind, and Body in the Healing of Trauma*. New York: Penguin, 2014.

Wang, Wayne, dir. *Coming Home Again*. Based on an essay by Chang-rae Lee. Written by Wayne Wang and Chang-rae Lee. Starring Justin Chon and Jackie Chung. A Center for Asian American Media Production. San Francisco: Center for Asian American Media, 2019. https://vimeo.com/ondemand/cominghomeagain/.

Watson, Ivan. "China: The Electronic Wastebasket of the World." *CNN*, May 30, 2013. https://www.cnn.com/2013/05/30/world/asia/china-electronic-waste-e-waste/index.html/.

Weingast, Matty. *The First Free Women: Poems of the Early Buddhist Nuns*. Boulder: Shambhala, 2020.

Williams, Caroline Randall. "You Want a Confederate Monument? My Body Is a Confederate Monument." *New York Times*, June 26, 2020. https://www.nytimes.com/2020/06/26/opinion/confederate-monuments-racism.html/.

Wolpe, David. *Making Loss Matter: Creating Meaning in Difficult Times*. New York: Riverhead, 2000.

Yun, Je-kyoon, dir. *Ode to My Father*. Written by Su-jin Park and Je-kyoon Yun. Starring Hwang Jung-min et al. DVD. South Korea: CJ Entertainment, 2014.

Zitter, Jessica Nutik. *Extreme Measures: Finding a Better Path to the End of Life*. New York: Avery, 2017.

———. *Jessica Zitter* (website). https://jessicazitter.com/.

CPSIA information can be obtained
at www.ICGtesting.com
Printed in the USA
BVHW031254280421
606061BV00004B/100